THE BROWN
FOUNDATIONS OF GEOGRAPHY
SERIES

A GEOGRAPHY OF
transportation and
business logistics

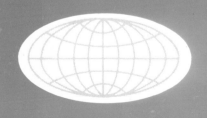

J. EDWIN BECHT

transportation and business logistics

THE BROWN
FOUNDATIONS OF GEOGRAPHY
SERIES

Consulting Editor
ROBERT H. FUSON
University of South Florida

A GEOGRAPHY OF

Agriculture
James R. Anderson, University of Florida
Transportation and Business Logistics
J. Edwin Becht, The University of Oklahoma
Plants and Animals
David J. de Laubenfels, Syracuse University
Geography
Robert H. Fuson, University of South Florida
The Atmosphere
John J. Hidore, Indiana University
Population and Settlement
Maurice E. McGaugh, Central Michigan University
Industrial Location
E. Willard Miller, The Pennsylvania State University
Water
Ralph E. Olson, The University of Oklahoma
Earth Form
Stuart C. Rothwell, University of South Florida
Minerals
Walter H. Voskuil, University of Nevada

THE BROWN
FOUNDATIONS OF GEOGRAPHY
SERIES

A GEOGRAPHY OF
transportation and business logistics

J. EDWIN BECHT
The University of Oklahoma

WM. C. BROWN COMPANY PUBLISHERS
DUBUQUE, IOWA

**THE BROWN
FOUNDATIONS OF GEOGRAPHY
SERIES**

Consulting Editor
ROBERT H. FUSON
University of South Florida

Copyright © 1970 by
Wm. C. Brown Company Publishers

ISBN 0–697–05152–8

Library of Congress Catalog Card Number: 70-118884

Printed in the United States of America.

Geography is one of man's oldest sciences, yet it is as new as the Space Age. Knowledge of the earth obtained from satellite photography and measurement, remote sensing of the environment, and by means of other sophisticated techniques are really but a stage in the evolutionary process that began with ancient man's curiosity about his surroundings. Man has always been interested in the earth and the things on it. Today this interest may be channeled through the discipline of geography, which offers one means of organizing a vast amount of physical and cultural information.

The **Brown Foundations of Geography Series** has been created to facilitate the study of physical, cultural, and methodological geography at the college level. The **Series** is a carefully selected group of titles that covers the wide spectrum of basic geography. While the individual titles are self-contained, collectively they comprise a modern synthesis of major geographical principles. The underlying theme of each book is to foster an awareness of geography as an imaginative, evolving science.

Preface

Geography is a combination of sciences and arts dealing with the differences from place to place as these differences might be interpreted by *man* as affecting *man* and his activities. Transportation is one of the relatively few truly great factors significantly affecting man which differs from place to place. At the same time, it is transportation that serves to equalize differences from place to place. The kinds and quality of transportation available to man form patterns of ebb and flow which are the arteries and veins of civilization. This pattern of peoples and goods in motion has, in turn, shaped the history of the world by setting certain bounds to man's activities and, at the same time, freeing man from local restrictions and giving time and place utility to his goods and services alike. Transportation, or lack of it, has determined the destiny of peoples and to date there is every indication that it will play an increasingly important role in man's ability to satisfy his wants and needs.

For the most part, transportation is considered as incidental to studies of international trade, marketing, manufacturing, engineering, urban growth and other facets of a total economy. When transportation is viewed as an adjunct to other functions there results, at best, a highly fragmented view of what are truly vitally important geographic, governmental, socio-economic, legalistic, technological, precedent-based, evolutionary phenomena which, in turn, shape the pattern of nearly all of man's activities.

Because of the importance to man of transportation throughout all of history, this study is intended to present today's pattern of goods and peoples in motion and an introduction to certain of the undergirding interpretations and understandings of geographic, economic, political, sociological, legal and technological differences from place to place which have produced these patterns. The purpose of the study is to provide guidelines to better predict/shape tomorrow's patterns. Admittedly, however, the study is atypical from a viewpoint of world transportation because it emphasizes transportation patterns as found within and radiating from the United States of America—the only nation in the world having a transportation system dominated by private enterprise. The United States, too, is the only nation in the world in which an excess of transportation capacity influences to such a high degree both the kinds and quality of transport modes and carrier competition within modes. Indeed, within the United States, the glut of transport facilities present governmental and resource allocation problems of such magnitude that only the nation's agricultural surpluses, urban blight, water and air pollution problems are comparable in magnitude and complexities.

Nevertheless, the study, for purposes of comparison, does deal with certain examples of transportation problems outside the United States. More specifically, it is hoped that the treatment provides concepts, interpretations and understandings of one of man's most vital, challenging, perplexing and vexing problem areas as he continues his struggle to serve his fellow man.

It is not feasible to give thanks and proper recognition to all of the sources which have shaped the ideas and concepts presented herein. Many thoughts, though now seemingly my own, originated in the literature and in discussions with such colleagues as B. J. Davis of Western Illinois University, Harry E. Colwell of the Texaco Corporation and many others. Special acknowledgments are made as footnotes. And, on a personal note, to Dorene—a wonderful name with wonderful meanings to me—my thanks for helping with manuscripts.

Contents

Chapter 1

Introduction to Transportation Patterns

Transportation Patterns

The patterns of transportation and business are kaleidoscopic and dynamic. Transportation and business logistics encompasses those activities involved in overcoming time and place discrepancies between where people are and where they may be needed or want to be and those time and place discrepancies between production and consumption, especially as these deal with the physical transport, handling and storing of products. In essence, the goal of business logistics as an area of study is to consider those techniques and steps which may be implemented to move an optimum mixture of raw materials, subassemblies and/or finished goods (along with the right people) to desired locations at those points in time which will maximize expected services or goods in terms of cost outlays.

Transportation Factors

The sets and subsets of factors shaping the gross transportation patterns of this nation (and much of the world) are legend and myriad in form. A list of these factors might well prove to be easier detailed than generalized, but even a list of these factors would be too voluminous to cover in a text of this size and plan. Thus, to deal in an effective, meaningful manner with such a constantly changing, evolutionary, revolutionary and vital subject, it is useful to reduce details to patterns; and, in turn, to account for the key factors producing those pattern sets and subsets while, at the same time, interpreting the significance of these patterns in the shaping of better means to meet and serve man's wants and needs.

Relationships between transportation (rail, highway, air, water and pipeline), on one hand, and terrain and climate conditions which may modify route orientations on the other, are but two kinds of relationships that must be considered along with cybernations between terminals, warehouses, commercial services, communications, markets, raw material sources, commodity flows, rates, routes, inter-regional and intra-company (corporation) traffic patterns, and packaging and handling requirements. And, as the location of plant, warehouse and market facilities affect the total efficiency of business logistics patterns, locational and spatial factors are especially pertinent in a study directed at the description and interpretation of the physical flow of people, goods and services.

Furthermore, most commodity traffic seeks destinations in response to many factors rather than to a certain factor such as, for example, distance. In this regard, the timing of a delivery may suggest that a train schedule may compel locating a certain factory further from its market than might otherwise seem desirable, and a need to store inbound shipments might result in their shipment by barge rather than by rail or truck. Thus, the complexities of transportation/business logistics when viewed broadly make a study of these subjects highly desirable. Yet, a broad approach to the study of transportation is fraught with dangers of incomplete explanation or misunderstanding. In any event, a search for those broad concepts with which to begin a study of transportation leads quickly to a recognition of routeways and routeway patterns.

The Routeway Concept

In short, a route is defined as a way or road for passage or travel. A highway, or railroad, or pipeline, or waterway, or airway is, by definition then, a route between any two points located on it. A routeway is defined, for purposes of this study, as consisting of two or more (at least roughly parallel) routes serving the same two points or terminals. Thus, routeways may, geographically speaking, be broad (or narrow) bands within which more than one route is used for the passage of people and/or freight. Indeed, some routeways may well be fan-shaped[1] or even radial.[2] For the most part, however, at least in the United States, routeways are band-shaped, consisting of at least two, but usually more than two, competing routes. Within each routeway competition may stem from within a carrier mode or between carrier modes.

1. An example of a fan-shaped routeway is that area served by the 34 granger and other rail lines radiating from Chicago, Illinois. (Granger lines are those rail lines initially developed to serve the agricultural markets of the Midwest.)
2. Examples of radial routeway patterns can be found in the transportation nets encompassing Paris, France, or Moscow, U.S.S.R.

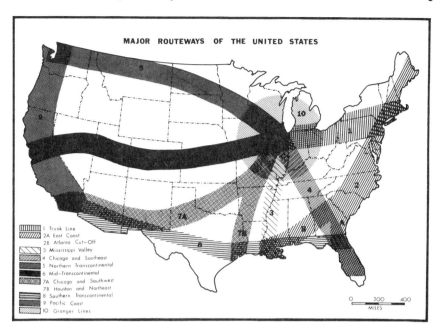

FIGURE 1.1. Major routeways of the United States.

Significantly, within the United States more than 85 percent of the population lives along the major routeways (see Figure 1.1) and probably more than 85 percent of all goods is shipped along these routeways. Even in regard to commodities from mines, forests and farms, applicable rates, terminals and schedules are so designed as to cause these shipments to gravitate to and move along the major routeways. These routeways form the gross transportation/business logistics framework within the contiguous 48 states. Similarly, a major share of both passengers and freight move along a major routeway(s). Some nations such as Canada may have only one major routeway while still other nations, as a matter of public policy, concentrate on developing and supporting one mode of transportation to the exclusion of other competing modes. Indeed, on no other continent has transportation competition between routes and between modes reached the level enjoyed in North America.

World-Wide Routeway Patterns

World-wide water (and air) routeway patterns have emerged (see Figure 1.2). Most ships and planes ply well-defined routes, even though they may seemingly be free to roam at will. Many of the same overriding considerations of domestic route development are at work in

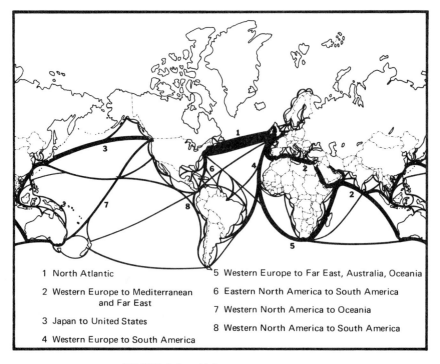

FIGURE 1.2. Major ocean routeways.

shaping international routes. In fact, other than to recognize the existence of international routeways, this reference will dwell chiefly on the patterns and their causes found within the 48 contiguous states of the United States.

Elements of a Routeway System

The patterns of routeways and routeway systems are the result of many forces. Most of the forces which produced present patterns are still operative and still changing so that the patterns themselves are in a state of flux and it seems destined that they will always be undergoing change. The dynamic nature of routeways and the reasons for their continuing change are worthy of consideration and are, of course, to be found in the characteristics of the element making up a transportation/business logistics pattern. The elements to be considered are discussed under the following headings:

I. Introduction to Transportation/Business Logistics Patterns
II. The Relative Decline in the Importance of Terrain and Climate in Shaping Transportation Patterns

III. Historical Backdrop to Today's Transportation and Business Logistics Patterns

IV. Introduction to the Carrier Operations—Bases of Routeway Patterns

V. Cybernetics and Business Logistics and Their Geographic Patterns

VI. Summary/Conclusions—An Evolving National Transportation/Business Logistics Pattern

Once each of the above major elements of a routeway system are examined in terms of their own patterns and properties, these elements are again related to the Gross Transportation/Business Logistics Patterns to form A Geography of Transportation and Business Logistics.

The Relative Decline in the Importance of Terrain and Climate in Shaping Transportation Patterns

It is difficult to place too much importance upon terrain and climate in the development of routeway patterns. Large land masses contain a diversity of terrain forms and climatic areas. Many of these, such as the Rocky Mountains in North America and the tundra climate areas, are physical barriers limiting ingress and egress. Other regions provide streams and lakes, waterway-favorable-grades, or some other salutary characteristics. Significantly, most terrain and climate factors, both favorable and unfavorable, tend to abet or hinder all forms of transportation alike. However, terrain and climate factors may well cause a certain transport mode to be used; i.e., planes in the Canadian bush, or Australian, outback. But, it is important that where roads are difficult to build, pipelines and airfields, too, are likely to be costly —even with modern machines and engineering technology.

In the past, land clearance and grading and draining the right-of-way have been the most costly aspects of transportation development. Engineering technology can now cut roads through sections of the Rockies at less cost than it takes to prepare a roadbed through the swamps and bayous of Louisiana or the faulted clay flats of the Texas coastal plain. Technology can level Appalachian mountains for airfields (such as at Charleston, West Virginia, or Pittsburgh) about as cheaply as drainage and ballast can be developed on the lake plains around Chicago. Probably the real difference costs today, in terms of transportation development, are found in the areas of land acquisition, property compensation, and in the foundation and surfacing materials to be used. And, especially in the case of the United States, the latter factors are growing faster in terms of costs than are those costs attendant with clearance, grading and drainage.

Impact of Increasing Land Values

Increasing land values (especially within the terminal metropolitan areas and along the major routeways), increasing population, and heavy industrialization have combined to produce a paucity of low-cost land for additional transportation facilities where they are needed most. In some areas, land is so scarce and costly as to preclude the use of some forms of transportation. For example, in Joliet, Illinois, a major firm receives delivery of phosphate rock by water at least in part due to the cost of acquiring enough land for switching and holding tracks which rail deliveries would necessitate. In such cases the use of trucks usually requires even more land. The only alternative, at present, is an inordinate effort devoted to scheduling the arrival and departure of trains and trucks which, costwise, is prohibitive.

Terrain, Climate, and Right-of-Way Cost Factors

Terrain determines gradients, alignment, and distance of transportation routes, unless these factors are overcome by using earth-moving equipment or tunnel-boring techniques. Climate, too, may limit use of a route seasonally such as forcing the closing of navigation on the Great Lakes and Upper Mississippi and Missouri Rivers for some five months each year. Similarly, snow in mountain passes may well close a route for several months annually. Hence, even though initial costs may seem high, it may actually cost less to tunnel through a mountain than to keep highways or tracks free of winter snows. In contrast, more powerful engines, greater range and altitude capabilities and electronic navigation aids have largely freed aircraft from limitations of climate and the widespread use and stationing of plows, graders, and salt-cinder-sand equipment are serving to keep traffic moving during winter months. Still, today, low grades through mountains, favorable bridge sites across streams, good natural harbors, and open rights-of-way into metropolitan areas are all powerful factors shaping transportation route patterns or alignments. Warm currents keep some ports free from ice, mountain ranges give rise to adiabatically warmed air masses melting winter snows, ridge routes provide well-drained rights-of-way requiring fewer bridges, and valley routes usually mean less cutting and filling. All of these natural features may, however, have disadvantages in terms of serving a given geographic area.

For example, it is difficult for valley farms to be served by a rail or highway route on a ridge and the opposite is often equally true. Snowfall and ice in the upper Midwest, Great Lakes, New England, and upper passes of the Rockies demand expensive wintertime maintenance measures. The use of snowplows and salt may determine the type of road metal to be used and the kinds of shoulders to be developed. For example, the kinds of grasses, or lack of grass, used on shoulders may well be set by the use of salt to free roads of snow and ice. The effects of freezing and thawing also add to the cost of road construction and maintenance in these areas. The prevention of damage from frost heave requires much deeper ballast and heavier road metal than otherwise would be required either by terrain, soil, or climate. In some areas gravel roads are used and a reduction in road speeds, damage from flying rocks, and periodic grading are all accepted as "trade-off" cost factors. Adiabatic heating often indicates areas of dry climates which, without irrigation, add little in the way of traffic to the carriers traversing the area.

Airport Locations

Historically, terrain and climate have played a key role in air travel. The foggy Appalachians, especially during periods of the year when quick successions of cyclonic storms with icing conditions are prevalent, were at one time known as the "graveyard of the airways." As pointed out, with the advent of more powerful engines and electronic navigational aids the adage no longer applies to commercial aviation, but the dangers are still inherent and definitely affect light aviation. Similarly, the high Rockies with their strong wind currents may limit aviation diurnally as well as seasonally. Thus, even though most commercial aviation now flies above terrain and climate obstacles, air routes for light aviation still may adhere to or follow passes through mountain barriers.

Airport construction, as pointed out, must be responsive, at least in terms of construction and operational costs. Topography, soils, water and fog (including smog and haze) are all to be considered in locating airports. But, due to a lack of land within reasonable distances to downtown metropolitan areas, cities find that it is cheaper to build land such as at Kennedy Airport in New York[1] or Meigs Field[2] in Chicago, or to bridge rivers and build in a different state such as was done in locating the Greater Cincinnati, Ohio, airport in Kentucky. Still other cities have found it expedient to literally knock the top off of mountains such as was done in Charleston, West Virginia. Los Angeles built their airport on a coastal plain not only for topographic reasons but to capitalize as much as possible on local land/sea breezes to aid in the dissipation of smog and haze. Houston, Texas, built a new Intercontinental Airport over 30 miles north of downtown Houston and over

---

1. Kennedy Airport was built by filling in coastal marsh.
2. Meigs Field is located on a man-made island in Lake Michigan.

40 miles north of the older Houston International Field, not only to avoid air traffic congestion and to find a sufficiently large tract of consolidated, undeveloped land but to secure a location in which operations could be carried out on some 30 to 35 additional fog- (smog)-free days (as compared with the older airfield located southeast of downtown Houston and close to the ship channel industries). Today, the search is on for promising sites which will handle supersonic planes. The center of Lake Michigan and the Florida Everglades are two sites being discussed—both present major construction and conservation problems.

Pipeline Orientations

Distance, terrain and rights-of-way are also important in pipeline orientations. Flow factors per linear mile determine pumping pressures unless some major elevation differences are involved. In pipeline locations, usually the shortest distance is the lowest in terms of operating costs. As traffic is usually one way the shortest route from collection-loading points convenient to producing fields or plants and markets to be served can be planned without consideration of backhaul advantages as is the case with vehicular or flight transportation. The number of pumping stations required to serve a line are more a function of pressure, viscosity and spacing than a function of terrain, as siphoning principles serve to draw liquid pipeline loads across rugged terrain. Even in the case of viscosity, with a technical ability to heat pipeline metal, climate is no longer *the* limiting factor that it has been. For, in the past, the relation of viscosity to climate has been (and still is, but to a lesser degree) an important consideration in the determination of pipeline depths to avoid permafrost zones, or even winter freeze layers in areas of extreme continental climates. Thus, today, pipeline insulation and/or electrical heating are important considerations especially in the Arctic fields of Alaska, Siberia, and northern European Russia. Toward this end considerable progress has been made for the development of techniques to keep the "skin" of pipelines warm (see Figure 2.1).

Topography and Waterways

In orienting canals or channelizing rivers, differences in elevation are important as are adequate reservoirs to assure year-round navigation (except as low temperatures and accompanying ice may bar traffic). Differences in elevation are normally surmounted by the construction of locks. The only, and in most cases unlikely, alternatives are a circuitous route or the use of elevators (inclined planes). Examples of the

FIGURE 2.1. Japanese worker checks tubing grounding on electric heating system for pipelines. This particular illustration shows the SECT (Skin Electric Current Tracing) system. This system offers new possible solutions to the problems of maintaining fluid viscosities in Alaska and other cold regions. (Photograph courtesy of Donald F. Othmer, Distinguished Professor, The Polytechnic Institute, Brooklyn, New York, and **Chemical Week,** June 14, 1969, p. 41.

latter are to be found in the canal system of the great European plain, especially as it traverses the Polish sector of that plain.

The number and height of locks to be used in a given waterway are determined by the following:

1. Stream and terrain pattern to include
2. Water reservoir potential
3. Kind, size and frequency of traffic
4. Elevation differences to be overcome

Navigating through locks adds risks, increases operational expense in terms of time, and requires more costly equipment.[3] In navigating

---

3. Passing through a lock usually requires anywhere from 45 minutes to two hours. Thus, locking operations alone on a tow northbound up the Ohio River, with its numerous locks (and dams), may total three to four 24-hour workdays.

locks, the pilot must exercise extreme caution as there is always a danger of lock, towboat or barge damage, accompanied by the extreme chance that the downstream locks might be destroyed spilling the vessel and/or tow downstream on the crest of a wall of water. In this connection the force of a vessel or tow in motion and weighing thousands of tons must always be kept in mind. Then, too, the construction of barges or vessels designed to withstand the pressure of water lifting heavy loads in them means more expensive hulls and internal reinforcement, thus adding to their construction costs.

Base Materials

The availability of soil and other materials for base materials varies from place to place. Soils vary in their firmness in terms of adequacy to serve as subgrade or roadbeds of railways, airports and highways. In vast areas such as the Pampas of Argentina, the Great Plains of North America, and the Steppes of European USSR, there are shortages of materials suitable for base construction.

Similarly, dam and canal construction require impervious soils that will minimize seepage or provide firm footings for locks and dams. Acid soils, too, are to be avoided as they add maintenance costs in terms of the construction metals used or rendered inoperative due to corrosive effects of soil acids. Even where rock formations are available, they are usually more expensive to use than satisfactory soils, if available.

All in all, modern day earth-moving equipment can be used to remove huge volumes of soil[4] to overcome the differences of base material availability from place to place. Still, long reaches of railroad tracks in the US are now on materials hauled hundreds of miles.[5]

Harbor Features

Natural terrain features which either in and of themselves form natural harbors, or which permit man to construct breakwaters, locks, or other terminal characteristics are among the strongest physical factors influencing transportation focal points. Still there are far more potential ports than are developed and used. Indeed, most ocean traffic moves between a relatively few leading ports having been attracted by productive hinterlands, rate structures, terminal equipment, ancillary commercial activities, or port investments. In fact, demands exist on such relatively few ports that it is a shortage of waterfront land, rather

---

4. The High Aswan Dam construction called for the removal, treatment, and replacement of sands 15 miles by 3 miles to an average depth of 400 feet.

5. Nearly one rail car out of every 40 hauls company materials to either maintain or improve tracks, roadbeds, or terminal facilities.

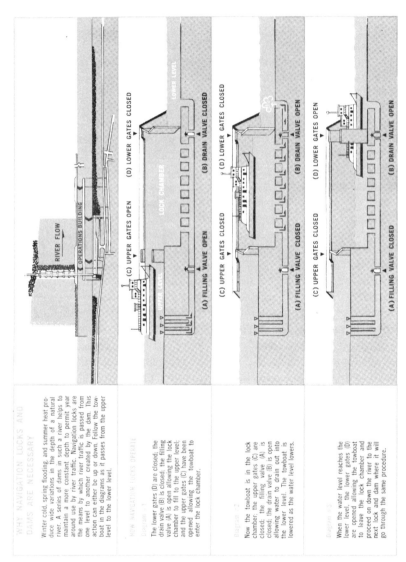

FIGURE 2.2.

Source: *Big Load Afloat*, a publication of The American Waterways Operators, Inc., Washington, D. C., 1965, pp. 42-43.

WHY NAVIGATION LOCKS AND DAMS ARE NECESSARY

Winter cold, spring flooding, and summer heat produce wide variations in the depth of a natural river. A series of dams in such a river helps to maintain a more constant depth to permit year around use by river traffic. Navigation locks are the means by which river traffic is passed from one level to another created by the dam. This action can either be up or down. Follow the towboat in the diagrams as it passes from the upper level to the lower level.

HOW NAVIGATION LOCKS OPERATE

Diagram 1

The lower gates (D) are closed; the drain valve (B) is closed; the filling valve (A) is open allowing the lock chamber to fill to the upper level; and the upper gates (C) have been opened allowing the towboat to enter the lock chamber.

Diagram 2

Now the towboat is in the lock chamber; the upper gates (C) are closed; the filling valve (A) is closed; the drain valve (B) is open allowing water to drain out into the lower level. The towboat is lowered as the water level lowers.

Diagram 3

When the water level reaches the lower level, the lower gates (D) are opened allowing the towboat to leave the lock chamber and proceed on down the river to the next lock and dam where it will go through the same procedure.

RIVER FLOW

OPERATIONS BUILDING

(C) UPPER GATES OPEN   (D) LOWER GATES CLOSED

LOCK CHAMBER

UPPER LEVEL   LOWER LEVEL

(A) FILLING VALVE OPEN   (B) DRAIN VALVE CLOSED

(C) UPPER GATES CLOSED   (D) LOWER GATES CLOSED

(A) FILLING VALVE CLOSED   (B) DRAIN VALVE OPEN

(C) UPPER GATES CLOSED   (D) LOWER GATES OPEN

(A) FILLING VALVE CLOSED   (B) DRAIN VALVE OPEN

than safe anchorage area, that limits and hinders further industrialization in and around such port areas as New York, Philadelphia, New Orleans, and Houston.

Good natural harbors, which provide shelter from wind and rough open water for deep-draft vessels (over 27 feet), are not evenly distributed. Much of the coasts of Africa and western South America have a paucity of good natural harbors. For the most part, man-made breakwaters or lightering from ships anchored offshore are but examples of make-shift measures adopted in the absence of natural features favorable for port development.

By and large there are two chief categories of good natural ports: those along coast lines of fairly recent tectonic activities, such as the San Francisco Bay and Puget Sound areas, and those ports along coast lines of submergence such as the ports on Chesapeake Bay. A third good port category are those encompassed by atolls—the latter, although useful for naval vessels, are seldom of great value as commercial ports because of their small hinterlands and relatively isolated locations.

Even though there are numerous ports along such shorelines of emergence as the East Florida and Texas Gulf Coasts, most of these ports are more man-made than natural. Most of these ports, unless scoured by a major river (i.e., Jacksonville, Florida—St. John's River and New Orleans—Mississippi River), require initial and maintenance dredging. Even they are most difficult to make and to maintain with sufficient depth for deeper-draft (over 27 feet) vessels. Only the ports of Houston, New Orleans and Mobile along the entire Gulf Coast can handle the largest tankers or ore ships. Even at these ports, the largest ships must off-load before entering and top-off as they leave the port and all three have difficulty handling the longest vessels. Similarly, almost without exception, lake and river ports require dredging and/or breakwater construction. Illustrations of the latter are such noteworthy lake ports as Chicago, Illinois; Cleveland and Toledo, Ohio; Erie, Pennsylvania; and others.

Only along the Arctic coasts of Alaska, Siberia, Canada, around Antarctica, in the Great Lakes, and on norther reaches of rivers in North America and Eurasia does seasonal ice preclude navigation. Throughout these areas improvements in the size of equipment and in ice-breaking techniques are more and more effective in minimizing the economic impact of seasonal limitations on water movements. (See Figure 2.3)

In common with other forms of transport terminal development the natural, physical attributes of a port area are chiefly permissive and are not the only considerations. In port areas the problems of land acquisition, property compensation, and access to and from the docks are equally pressing considerations and, as pointed out above, in certain

FIGURE 2.3. S. S. Manhattan opening a new transportation route which promises significant shifts in tanker requirements and routes. Photograph courtesy Humble Oil and Refining Co., September, 1969.

port areas (such as New York, San Francisco, New Orleans, and Chicago) these factors may well constitute major limitations to contined port developments. The better the natural port features, the more likely these nonphysical considerations will become major limitations.

Aerial Tramways and Conveyor Belts

Where land requirements may preclude interference with its use, or where terrain is so rugged that leveling costs are prohibitive, aerial tramways are used effectively. Sites for cable towers or angle stations are the only impingement on land uses. Thus, in heavily industrialized areas, rugged terrain, or where mining areas are frequently shifted, aerial tramways are effective. Cement, ores, rock, wood chips, and other similar commodities are especially well adapted to this type of carrier.

Conveyor belts, sometimes used to cross heavy traffic highways or other barriers, by and large over a long distance and for large scale operations, require nearly as much "rights-of-way" area as a single-track railroad. This factor, combined with technical difficulties connected with belting materials, limits their use to special purposes or situations.

Transport Capacities

Transport capacities are usually related to terrain and climate. Where terrain and climate make transportation facilities costly to develop and maintain, there is usually a relatively sparse population. Thus, in most such areas, *permanent* transport facilities enjoy a relatively low standard in terms of investment. Where terrain and climate favor transport facility construction, usually minimum standards are high. Thus, if minimum standards are realistic, in theory at least, transport facility costs should be about the same anywhere in the world. However, the general practice (need) of specifying standards to meet future requirements rather than merely meeting today's needs, results in widespread overbuilding, with very real attendant costs. These, then, become the real differences in transport facility construction costs from place to place. Thus, the prediction of demand becomes essential in the developing of an optimum transportation system.

Accessibility to Transport Routes

Feeder routes to and from transport facilities vary from place to place and must be considered in connection with a transport system. In some areas such as swampy, coastal reaches, cross-country movement is difficult if not impossible, even though main roads may transverse the area. This is especially true where roads may be elevated; i.e., South Florida, the Netherlands, etc. In mountainous areas where roads are built on well-drained gravels it may be relatively easy to get on and off roads, but cross-country movement is limited. In certain other areas, cross-country movement may be excellent, but due to roads elevated above occasional floods (i.e., Lower Mississippi Valley and the Po Valley of Italy) it is difficult (and expensive) to prepare points at which to enter or leave major highways.

In much of the United States, however, it is feasible to get on and off major highways. So easy is it, in fact, that in cases where entry and departures are not controlled highways become clogged and dangerous due to traffic entering or leaving.[6] To avoid this, limited access highways are used—even though expensive in terms of land requirements, construction costs, and their barrier effect on cross movements.

Conclusions

Terrain and climate as reflected in transport costs do not now produce as great differences from place to place as has been the case in the past. Decreases in differences are relative rather than absolute in that transport construction technology has combined with the press of population, land acquisition, consolidation problems, and property costs to effect, geographically, more nearly equal transport development costs. Then, too, where terrain and climate might otherwise dictate more costly construction factors, lower minimum construction standards usually apply which, in turn, serve to equalize transport facility construction costs.

The total effect of these factors is not to deprecate the importance of terrain and climate in terms of their influence on transport patterns, but rather to point up and emphasize that in terms of cost per unit of transportation effort, one total effect of climate and weather is that of equalizing the investment needed to develop adequate transport for a given region as compared with most other regions.

6. Old US Highway No. 1 between Washington, D. C. and Baltimore, Maryland averages an entrance/exit every 45 yards. The Washington, D. C.-Baltimore Parkway (a limited access highway) was built to remove traffic pressures, which when combined with problems relating to unlimited access, made old US 1 both dangerous and congested to a point where traffic simply could not move.

Chapter **3**

Historical Backdrop to Today's Transportation and Business Logistic Patterns

During this century much of the world has witnessed a revolution in transportation. This is especially true of the United States. All aspects of man's activities have been profoundly affected. Economic development of regions, military postures of nations, political decisions and social conditions (local as well as national) have all been shaped and reshaped depending upon changes in transportation patterns. As late as the 1920's, in the most advanced countries, railroads played the dominant role. Domestically, water, both ocean and inland, played supplementing roles at best and only in international trade was ocean transport important. Locally, as in the North Sea, Sea of Japan, and rivers and streams of Western Europe, and on a few selected streams elsewhere in the world, inland waterways were important.

In the United States, however, by 1895, inland water transport was already quiescent and destined to remain so until World War I breathed new life into the shallow-draft waterway industry, and railroads were essentially the only means of moving both people and freight throughout most of the United States. So dependent had this nation become on rail transport that when the railroads failed to build and add rolling stock fast enough to keep pace with peaks in the economy, the economic depression of 1906-07 resulted.

Thus, by way of backdrop, if one is to understand the patterns of transportation currently shaping events in and for the United States, it is essential to begin with the turn of the twentieth century, when the country was virtually a one-carrier nation. This period of the nation's history began with the temporary demise of inland water transportation in 1890 and was destined to last until the early 1920's when water, highway, pipeline and air all began to move important volumes of the nation's commerce.

Decline of the River Boat: 1890-1920

The widespread stream system of the United States is readily adaptable to river navigation; indeed, these streams were widely used during the early settlement years. Especially, beginning in 1811, there began a widespread as well as intensive use of American waterways, reaching a climax in 1879 when the jetties at the mouth of the Mississippi were completed. In that year, more than one million tons were handled at the port of St. Louis alone. However, after 1879, a decline set in and by 1905 St. Louis handled only 141,000 tons.[1]

Though the railroad emancipated transportation from many limitations of topography and climate, certain economic forces and social values were engendered which caused the nation's public and its political leaders to seek out competing forms of carriers.

Geographic and Economic Bases for the Return of Inland Water Transportation and Other Carrier Types

The transportation crisis of 1906-07 was one of the outstanding factors reawaking the American public to a need for a development of water and other types of carriers. However, few men indeed could foresee any other possibility than water transport at this time. Numerous editorials appeared in papers across the nation proposing water transportation as a means of circumventing the box car shortage of those critical years. *The Wall Street Journal* of January 1, 1907, reported, "But for the car shortage our business expansion might have increased twenty-five percent above that of 1905."[2] Farmers and industrialists throughout the nation were irked at the lack of transportation; grain was stored on the ground, coal stockpiles were not maintained, and wholesalers, as well as retailers, deplored the lack of transport services.

During those years, as is the case today, there was an increase in population, as well as a high level of business activity. Heavy mercantile travel resulted in the further expansion of already burgeoning jobbing and wholesale lines. The West had been won; ideal weather was beneficial to crops and to commerce. Orders for coal, iron and steel increased far beyond what were usually considered reasonable commitments by the carriers involved. Exports to Europe grew. Grain, lumber and leather tonnages were especially large. Furthermore, there was a heavy cotton crop. To sum up the effects of the transportation crisis *The Wall Street Journal* of August 22, 1906, stated, "The railroads are at their wits' end to know how they will take care of it all."[3] The

---

1. *St. Louis Globe Democrat*, February 17, 1909, p. 9.
2. *The Wall Street Journal*, January 1, 1907, p. 12.
3. *The Wall Street Journal*, August 22, 1906, p. 12.

increase in the wealth of the nation was unprecedented; 1906 bank clearings gained 11.3 percent over 1905; foreign commerce increased 16 percent in exports and 9 percent in imports.[4] During 1907 editorials appearing in the *St. Louis Globe Democrat,* and other papers pointed out such economic data as: (1) the nation's annual growth in population of approximately two million people, (2) the doubling of iron production in the period 1900-1906, and (3) the huge increases in cotton and grain production, especially for exports.[5] A lack of transport was the chief factor limiting faster economic growth.

Similar conditions existed well into 1907; and, though the transport crisis had eased somewhat by December 1, 1907, an impression had been made upon the public favorable to government aid in forestalling another such crisis in the country's transport system.[6]

The Panama Canal

Business men of many midwestern cities envisioned in the plans for the opening of a canal across the isthmus of Panama an opportunity for markets, via all-water transportation, along the West Coast of the United States, along the West Coast of South America, and in the Far East. They pictured their cities and factories augmenting many Eastern and European suppliers. It was with these markets in mind that enterprising business men sent delegates to numerous "Deep Water Conventions."[7] Especially did businessmen of the port of New Orleans want a well-developed and efficient network of water routes to accommodate potential canal traffic. With Panama Canal trade in mind the Port of New Orleans sponsored their Deep Water Convention in 1909.[8]

Planning Associations and Conventions

Interested persons throughout the country formed associations to work for wise watershed development. Typical of the associations organized to improve the multiple uses of rivers were the Rivers and Harbors Congress, the Upper Mississippi Valley Improvement Association. The Lakes to the Gulf Deep Water Association, Missouri River Improvement League, Deep Waterways Convention Series, Mississippi Rivers Committee, and the Greater Ohio Valley Association.

---

4. *St. Louis Globe Democrat, op. cit.*
5. Congressional hearings attendant with the passage of the Hepburn Act of 1906 and the Mann-Elkins Act of 1910.
6. *Ibid.*
7. E. L. Bogart, *Economic History of the American People* (Longmans, Green and Co., New York, 1930), p. 788.
8. *Ibid.*

Position of Federal Government

Both Presidents Roosevelt and Taft aided the movement to develop inland waterways. Perhaps their principal aid was to bring the issue before the public. Opportunities to do this were afforded by the well-publicized river trips which each president made. Both trips were from St. Louis to New Orleans and included large parties composed of cabinet and congress members, governors of states, newspapermen and magazine editors. In many ways these trips were comparable to President Nixon's 1969 trip around the world, as for weeks before and after the journeys papers were filled with such headlines as "Flagship Oleander Overhauled for President," "Governors Mingle Talking Waterway," "Taft Proposes Waterway Bonds," etc. Pictures of packets covered entire pages, and many editorials treated the subject.

President Roosevelt took a very definite stand for government aid to potential water shippers and set forth his ideas very clearly in his Memphis address, "Our National Inland Waterways Policy," on October 4, 1907.[9] In this address he stated low-cost transportation to be a necessity for modern civilization. As regards rail rates he said, "Wherever a navigable river runs along a railroad the problem of regulating rates on the railroad becomes far easier because river regulation is rate regulation. Year by year transportation problems become more acute. The National Government should undertake this work!" President Theodore Roosevelt also took some positive action in that he appointed what he called the Inland Waterways Commission in 1907, charged with making a complete investigation and instructed to report their findings to him and to Congress.

Conservationists' Arguments

Shortly after the turn of the century the movement to conserve our natural resources provided a further impetus to eventual government improvements of the nation's waterways. President Theodore Roosevelt and Governor Pinchot of Pennsylvania were among the outstanding leaders in this movement. Roosevelt's "Inland Waterways Commission" recognized the possibilities of manifold results in its preliminary report of March, 1908.[10] The committee stated that improvements of navigation on inland waterways, in the main, affect favorably the purity of the waters and the regularity of the supply. They noted that there was an increasing pollution of rivers by soil wash, and human wastes, and that diminished water supplies in late summer indicated a need for

9. *Ibid.*
10. Bogart, *op. cit.*, p. 788.

reforestation. Forests and dams, in addition to aiding river transportation, provide for storage of floodwaters.[11]

In 1907 the Lakes to the Gulf Association asked President Roosevelt to go down the Mississippi River from St. Louis to New Orleans to study river conditions. This he did, accompanied by 17 governors, stopping enroute to address the Deep Waterways Convention in Memphis. In his Memphis address, "Our National Inland Waterways Policy," he developed to a high degree the argument of multiplicity of advantages.[12]

Industrial Needs and Success of Inland Water Transportation in Europe

Following the recession of late 1907 many industrialists sought markets overseas. In examining their production costs and in making comparisons with European conditions, transportation stood out as a factor in placing the American manufacturers at a disadvantage. H. B. Fuller, in a study for the Inland Waterways Commission, reported in 1912, "The railroad facilities of this country approximate only 60 percent of the development necessary for properly handling our freight. The present system of transportation is not only inadequate for our present needs, but its future development cannot keep pace with the growing demands of our industrial life."[13]

Along with the Rhine River, Germany, France, and Belgium made the Ghent-Tennenzen, the Kaiser-Wilhelm, the Canal du Nord, and the Canal St. Quentin busy freight highways. Though admitting more favorable conditions in Europe, Senator Theodore E. Burton (Ohio), Chairman of the Inland Waterways Commission, noted that the American potential, due to the vast area served by rivers, to be as great as Europe's[14] Europe's great advantage, Fuller pointed out, was that they completed one project before beginning another.[15]

Big Stick Over Railroads

Though there were some advocates of waterway development that thought they should not be used as a club to keep down rail rates, many did argue this factor as a point for favoring federal legislation. Senator Burton expressed his feelings against this argument. He said, "Moreover, we should not consider our rivers merely as weapons with which to hold the railroads in subject. The courts and Interstate Com-

11. *St. Louis Globe Democrat, op. cit.*
12. *Ibid.*
13. U. S. Government "Inland Waterway Commission Report," 1912.
14. *Ibid.*
15. *Ibid.*

merce Commission exist for that purpose. Our rivers should be improved for the development of commerce and not for the purpose of controlling railroad rates, as has frequently been done in the past."

That many proponents for deep waterways were attempting to control railroads is true. For example, this theme was one President Roosevelt proposed in his Memphis address. Still others pointed out that railroads had been unfairly subsidized by land grants; therefore, in order to repair past damages the government should provide generous aid to inland navigation. Also, while the decline in the use of water transportation was in part due to the natural growth and extension of railways, there was also evidence that railway interests had in some instances been successfully directed against the normal maintenance and development of water traffic by control of waterfronts and terminals, by acquistion or control of competing canals and vessels, by discriminating tariffs, by rebates, by the temporary expedient of having profits away from parallel water routes support low rates along them, and by adverse placement of tracks and structures, so as to prevent a longtime water development. Due to credence given these practices the "Big Stick" argument was effective in arousing a certain amount of public and political support.

Legislation Designed to Aid Inland Navigation

A mass of bills concerning inland waterways was approved by Congress during the period 1900 to 1920. Many more bills were introduced that received little or unfavorable attention from Congress. Several examples of the more outstanding bills passed are mentioned. An act authorizing the condemnation of lands or easements needed in connection with works of rivers and harbor improvements at the expense of persons, companies, or corporations was approved May 16, 1906. On August 24, 1912, President Taft signed a bill giving coastwise trade free access to the Panama Canal. Naturally this bill raised the hopes of midwest manufacturers and farmers that the Panama Canal would be a boon to them. It was short lived, however, as President Wilson signed a bill repealing the access bill on June 15, 1914.

Typical of the bills introduced to Congress was one by Ransdell of Louisiana and Moore of Pennsylvania for the general improvement of the waterways of the entire United States and its Territories. Senator Newlands was supported by President Wilson in his proposed amendment to the Rivers and Harbors Bill of 1914 providing for a national commission to coordinate various improvements and to stop waste. Collectively, the total of such bills introduced was considerable and served to keep transportation issues in front of Congress and the public.

Factors Retarding Aid to River Transportation

In spite of the foregoing events neither government nor private capital provided much aid to water carriers until pressures of World War I and the advent of truck transportation combined to renew interest in the potentials of barge traffic. Though not numerous, the reasons for this failure are clear. Also, as pointed out in the "Big Stick" viewpoint, the railroads were powerful and in key areas used their strength to forestall government interference with their near monopoly of transportation in the United States. First, it should be pointed out that for all but a handful of commodities rail service is far superior to water transport. Frequency of schedules, speed, less need for transshipment, early unlimited geographic coverage, the absence of seasonal influences, specialized equipment, larger capital investment, and aggressive rate structures doomed river traffic to a "poor-brother" status, at best, at an early date. In fact, only since 1935 has newly designed equipment been developed to enable water carriers to compete effectively in the hauling of even certain of the basic bulk commodities and only since the 1947 Mechling Supreme Court Decision have rate structures been permissive in regard to water development. Furthermore, one of the most potent factors that prevented adequate government aid to river transportation was the unscientific method of river and harbor improvements. Instead of concentrating improvements on only the large streams, more nearly capable of repaying invested funds, money was appropriated over a wide area and sums were thrown away on many projects before their time. Examples of such projects were the attempts to make navigable the Big Sandy River in West Virginia and the Upper Trinity River in Texas. In fact, in the general River and Harbor Act of 1910, 296 out of 391 Congressional districts of the United States received an appropriation. The $52 million of that bill was regarded as a political fund to be circulated in different parts of the country rather than be applied to the real needs of watershed or water transportation development.[16]

Beginning of Government Operations and Multi-Mode Operations Along the Routeways

The congestion of freight on the railways of the United States and the demand for more adequate transportation service led to an increased utilization of inland waterways during 1917 as a war measure.

During the year 1917, St. Paul, Moline, Rock Island, Davenport, and Muscatine, on the upper Mississippi River, were building modern terminal facilities; Tuscaloosa and Mobile were constructing and improving facilities. Memphis voted $500,000 in bonds for the construction of a

---

16. *Ibid.*

terminal at that point, and at La Salle, Illinois, slips were built for the construction of towboats and barges.[17]

Also in 1917, the War Department placed barges in service on the upper Mississippi River and a water service was established between Florence, Alabama, and Peoria, Illinois. In addition, a fleet of barges and towboats was ordered to augment these facilities. With a shortage of cars in Louisiana, sugar was moved by barge from plantations to New Orleans. Work on a navigation channel from the Great Lakes to the Illinois River and then on to the Mississippi was renewed. At New Orleans a terminal and waterfront storage system (coordinating river, rail, and ocean transportation) was being developed. Modern river transportation had begun. Railroads were seemingly no longer destined to be the only important US transportation carrier.

In Conclusion

A whole series of needs (lessons learned when the nation lacked adequate competition in transportation) set the stage for the development, mostly by government subsidy, of today's competitive transport carriers opearing along the nation's routeways. The transportation crisis of 1906-1907, development of the Panama Canal, activities of interested associations, political interests of many statesmen (including President Theodore Roosevelt) industrialist's ambitions, successful examples set by Europe's river transport systems, a conservationist movement, and a supposed (or real) need of a "Big Stick" over railroads all combined to furnish necessary interest and machinery to continue working for rail competition (chiefly inland waterways) beginning with and following World War I. In brief, the stage had been well set before 1917; World War I but raised the curtain.

There seems little chance that again, as in 1906-1907, our economy will be stifled by failing to develop and protect all phases of our transportation industry.

Today's routeway pattern stems from this period in our nation's history (1897-1917) when there was but one carrier mode in operation. Today, in competition with the basic carrier, the railroads, there is strong competition from the barge, truck, air, and pipeline industries. A knowledge of basic carrier patterns is fundamental and requisite to the ultimate transport patterns emerging in this nation and, thus, are the subject of the next chapter.

---

17. Bogart, *op. cit.*

Chapter **4**

Introduction to Carrier Operations—
Bases of Routeway Patterns

The chief elements affecting the ebb and flow of commodities along the routeway pattern of a nation and of the world are the carriers. By mode, these carriers are

1. Railroad
2. Waterways—inland, coastal and ocean
3. Highway carriers
4. Air
5. Pipeline
6. Special or limited.

The Railroad Pattern

Beginning with the immediate pre-Civil War years up to 1945 railroads were the major hauler of both passengers and freight. However, with the advent of the automobile, by 1940 railroads were hauling less than 8 percent of intercity passengers (Table 4.1); nevertheless, as recently as 1953, the railroads were still hauling more than 50 percent of all intercity freight. By 1967 this percentage had dropped to 41.6, with trucks accounting for 22.1; pipelines, 20.5; Great Lakes, 6.2; Rivers and Canals, 9.4; air, 0.15 (Table 4.2).

World-wide, the investment made in a given type of carrier is usually a matter of national policy; competition, as a matter of course, is restricted. Not so in the United States where competition between and within carrier mode has been (and still is) extremely strong. As a matter of national policy, the different modes have been nurtured and protected in the interest of furthering and assuring competition. As a result, today carrier competition for an estimated $55 billion in freight charges is

TABLE 4.1

Intercity Travel by Modes
(Billions of Passenger-Miles)

| | TOTAL | | PRIVATE CARRIER | | | | | | PUBLIC CARRIER | | | | | | | | |
| | | | Auto | | Air | | Total | | Air | | Bus | | Rail | | Water | | Total | |
Year	Amount	%	Amount	%	Amount	%	Amount	%	Amount	%	Amount	%	Amount	%	Amount	%	Amount	%
1939	311.0	100	275.4	88.6	.1	-	275.5	88.6	.8	.3	9.5	3.0	23.7	7.6	1.5	.5	35.5	11.4
1940	330.3	100	292.7	88.6	.1	-	292.8	88.6	1.2	.4	10.2	3.1	24.8	7.5	1.3	.4	37.5	11.4
1941	371.7	100	324.0	87.2	.1	-	324.1	87.2	1.7	.5	13.5	3.6	30.6	8.2	1.8	.5	47.6	12.8
1942	324.2	100	244.1	75.3	.1	-	244.2	75.3	1.7	.5	21.3	6.6	55.1	17.0	1.9	.6	80.0	24.7
1943	295.7	100	176.0	59.5		-	176.0	59.5	2.0	.7	25.9	8.8	89.9	30.4	1.9	.6	119.7	40.5
1944	311.5	100	181.4	58.2		-	181.4	58.2	2.9	.9	27.3	8.8	97.7	31.4	2.2	.7	130.1	41.8
1945	347.6	100	220.3	63.4		-	220.3	63.4	4.3	1.2	27.4	7.9	93.5	26.9	2.1	.6	127.3	36.6
1946	427.0	100	324.0	75.8	.3	.1	324.3	75.9	7.2	1.7	26.9	6.3	66.3	15.5	2.3	.6	102.7	24.1
1947	428.9	100	347.8	81.1	.6	.1	348.4	81.2	7.1	1.7	24.8	5.8	46.8	10.9	1.8	.4	80.5	18.8
1948	440.7	100	365.0	82.8	.7	.2	365.7	83.0	6.8	1.5	24.6	5.6	41.9	9.5	1.7	.4	75.0	17.0
1949	479.4	100	409.4	85.4	.8	.2	410.2	85.6	7.8	1.6	24.0	5.0	36.0	7.5	1.4	.3	69.2	14.4
1950	504.8	100	438.3	86.8	.8	.2	439.1	87.0	9.3	1.8	22.7	4.5	32.5	6.5	1.2	.2	65.7	13.0
1951	571.2	100	498.1	87.2	.9	.2	499.0	87.4	12.0	2.1	23.6	4.1	35.3	6.2	1.3	.2	72.2	12.6
1952	614.3	100	539.2	87.7	1.0	.2	540.2	87.9	13.3	2.2	24.7	4.0	34.7	5.7	1.4	.2	74.1	12.1
1953	651.4	100	575.8	88.4	1.2	.2	577.0	88.6	16.2	2.5	24.4	3.7	32.3	5.0	1.5	.2	74.4	11.4
1954	669.9	100	597.1	89.1	1.4	.2	598.5	89.3	18.2	2.7	22.0	3.3	29.5	4.4	1.7	.3	71.4	10.7
1955	712.5	100	637.4	89.5	1.5	.2	638.9	89.7	21.3	3.0	21.9	3.1	28.7	4.0	1.7	.2	73.6	10.3
1956	747.4	100	669.7	89.6	1.6	.2	671.3	89.8	23.9	3.2	21.7	2.9	28.6	3.8	1.9	.3	76.1	10.2
1957	748.3	100	670.5	89.6	1.8	.2	672.3	89.8	26.3	3.5	21.5	2.9	26.3	3.5	1.9	.3	76.0	10.2
1958	759.9	100	684.9	90.1	2.1	.3	687.0	90.4	26.4	3.5	20.8	2.7	23.6	3.1	2.1	.3	72.9	9.6
1959	764.8	100	687.4	89.9	2.1	.3	689.5	90.2	30.5	3.9	20.4	2.7	22.4	2.9	2.0	.3	75.3	9.8
1960	783.7	100	706.1	90.1	2.3	.3	708.4	90.4	31.7	4.0	19.3	2.5	21.6	2.8	2.7	.3	75.3	9.6
1961	791.3	100	713.6	90.2	2.3	.3	715.9	90.5	32.3	4.0	20.3	2.6	20.5	2.6	2.3	.3	75.4	9.5
1962	818.1	100	735.9	90.0	2.7	.3	738.6	90.3	34.8	4.2	21.8	2.7	20.2	2.5	2.7	.3	79.5	9.7
1963	852.6	100	765.9	89.8	3.4	.4	769.3	90.2	39.4	4.7	22.5	2.6	18.6	2.2	2.8	.3	83.3	9.8
1964	895.5	100	801.8	89.5	3.7	.4	805.5	89.9	45.5	5.1	23.3	2.6	18.4	2.1	2.8	.3	90.0	10.1
1965	920.3	100	817.7	88.8	4.4	.5	822.1	89.3	53.7	5.9	23.8	2.6	17.6	1.9	3.1	.3	98.2	10.7
1966	971.1	100	856.4	88.2	5.7	.6	862.1	88.8	63.7	6.5	24.6	2.5	17.3	1.8	3.4	.4	109.0	11.2
1967	1,020.6	100	889.8	87.2	7.0	.7	896.8	87.9	80.2	7.9	24.9	2.4	15.3	1.5	3.4	.3	123.8	12.1
(p)1968	1,073.3	100	931.0	86.7	8.1	.8	939.1	87.5	93.0	8.7	24.5	2.3	13.2	1.2	3.5	.3	134.2	12.5

(p) TAA preliminary estimate.

Source: *Transportation: Facts and Trends* (Transportation Association of America, Washington, D. C., Sixth Edition, April 1969), p. 13.

extremely keen. Indeed, in the minds of many carriers and shippers alike, the number and kinds of transportation available in the United States today looms as a serious national problem in many ways comparable to agricultural surpluses.

The broad general coverage provided by the nation's railroads is well illustrated in Figure 4.1. All of the industrialized sections of the country are less than 25 miles from a rail line. Significantly, this does not mean that rail service is available within this distance, but at least at a feasible price, if warranted, switches and other terminal equipment could be installed as rights-of-way and trackage are available within 25 miles. The rail net of the United States as of 1966 is shown on Figure 4.2. By comparing this map with the Routeways of Figure 1.1, the importance of the United States rail system in providing the basic outline of the total routeway pattern is evident. In fact, operationally as well as historically, the rail system forms the backbone of the nation's major routeways.

TABLE 4.2

Intercity Freight by Modes* (*Including Mail & Express*)
(Billions of Ton-Miles)

	Rail Amount	%	Truck Amount	%	Oil Pipeline Amount	%	Great Lakes Amount	%	Rivers and Canals Amount	%	Air Amount	%	Total
								**		**			
1939	339	62.3	53	9.7	56	10.3	76	14.0	20	3.7	.01	00	544
1940	379	61.3	62	10.0	59	9.5	96	15.5	22	3.6	.02	00	618
1941	482	62.4	81	10.5	68	8.8	114	14.8	27	3.5	.02	00	772
1942	645	69.5	60	6.5	75	8.1	122	13.1	26	2.8	.04	00	928
1943	735	71.3	57	5.5	98	9.5	115	11.2	26	2.5	.05	00	1,031
1944	747	68.7	58	5.3	133	12.2	119	10.9	31	2.8	.07	.01	1,088
1945	691	67.2	67	6.5	127	12.4	113	11.0	30	2.9	.09	.01	1,028
1946	602	66.6	82	9.1	96	10.6	96	10.6	28	3.1	.08	.01	904
1947	665	65.3	102	10.0	105	10.3	112	11.0	35	3.4	.11	.01	1,019
1948	647	61.9	116	11.1	120	11.5	119	11.4	43	4.1	.15	.01	1,045
1949	535	58.3	127	13.8	115	12.5	98	10.7	42	4.6	.20	.02	917
1950	597	56.2	173	16.3	129	12.1	112	10.5	52	4.9	.30	.03	1,063
1951	655	55.6	188	16.0	152	12.9	120	10.2	62	5.3	.34	.03	1,177
1952	623	54.4	195	17.0	158	13.8	105	9.2	64	5.6	.34	.03	1,145
1953	614	51.0	217	18.0	170	14.1	127	10.6	75	6.2	.37	.03	1,203
1954	557	49.6	213	19.0	179	15.9	91	8.1	83	7.4	.38	.03	1,123
1955	631	49.5	223	17.5	203	15.9	119(105)	9.3	98(64)	7.7	.49	.04	1,274
1956	656	48.4	249	18.4	230	17.0	111(94)	8.2	109(74)	8.0	.58	.04	1,356
1957	626	46.9	254	19.0	223	16.7	117(101)	8.8	115(79)	8.6	.68	.05	1,336
1958	559	46.0	256	21.1	211	17.4	80(62)	6.6	109(73)	9.0	.70	.05	1,216
1959	582	45.3	279	21.7	227	17.7	80(68)	6.2	117(79)	9.1	.80	.06	1,286
1960	579	44.1	285	21.8	229	17.4	99(81)	7.5	121(82)	9.2	.89	.07	1,314
1961	570	43.5	296	22.7	233	17.8	87(67)	6.6	123(84)	9.4	1.01	.08	1,310
1962	600	43.8	309	22.5	238	17.3	90(66)	6.6	133(90)	9.7	1.30	.09	1,371
1963	629	43.3	336	23.1	253	17.4	95(68)	6.5	139(94)	9.6	1.30	.09	1,453
1964	666	43.2	356	23.1	269	17.4	106(73)	6.9	144(102)	9.3	1.50	.10	1,543
1965	709	43.3	359	21.9	306	18.7	110(76)	6.7	152(110)	9.3	1.91	.12	1,638
1966	751	43.0	381	21.8	333	19.1	116(81)	6.6	164(117)	9.4	2.25	.13	1,747
1967	731	41.6	389	22.1	361	20.5	109(74) #	6.2	165(118)	9.4	2.59	.15	1,758
1968 (p)	755	40.9	415	22.5	397	21.5	108(73) #	5.9	167(120) #	9.1	3.11	.17	1,845

* Includes both for-hire and private carriers. # Breakdown estimated by TAA. (p) Preliminary TAA estimate.
** See source data for figures in parenthesis, which are based on different reporting techniques.

Source: *Transportation: Facts and Trends* (Transportation Association of America, Washington, D. C., Sixth Edition, April 1969), p. 7.

Declining railroad-line mileage (See Table 4.3) should be interpreted as route abandonment. In addition, there has been a widespread abandonment of parallel trackage. The latter is not necessarily related to traffic volume, because numerous parallel tracks are no longer as important to safety and service levels as was formerly the case. Central-Traffic-Control (CTC) and other technological improvements have resulted in more efficient use of a single track than was formerly possible. Significantly, a chief cause for reducing line-haul mileages has been rail mergers which have made possible reductions in duplicate facilities (and have effected certain economies of scale). However, these reductions, although reducing track-line mileages have not reduced routeway mileages (See Table 4.3).

Originally, US railroads were mostly short, independent lines serving very specific markets (See Figure 4.3); although the original rails were built to serve as feeder lines, it soon became clear that railroads could best serve by providing through services. (See Figure 4.2). Thus, the nation's railroad system has undergone and is continuing to undergo consolidations, mergers and abandonments with irrepressible pressures to offer a single carrier name to ever larger service regions. Today such giants as the Penn Central, Norfolk and Western, Southern Pacific, Burlington Northern, and Santa Fe each serve areas approximating one-fourth of the nation. Such rail giants extend more than half-way east-west across the nation and, in the case of the Southern Pacific, from northern border to southern border.

The railroad net of the United States is truly a national system. Any shipper in the nation can load a railroad car(s) for movement, without break in bulk, to any rail point on the continent (except for a few miles of narrow gauge rails in Colorado and other isolated instances). Significantly, railroads in the United States, as a national system, are rapidly becoming a system providing special services. More and more railroads are moving toward special services in the areas of

1. Oversized (jumbo) cars specifically designed to move certain (or a few specialized) commodities
2. Trailer-on-Flatcar service (TOFC)

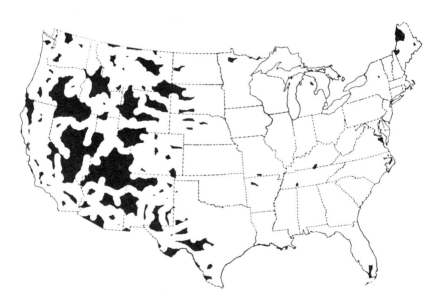

FIGURE 4.1. Only the areas shown in black are more than 25 miles (approximately one-half hour's drive) from a railroad. Students of geography will recognize that these are areas of sparse population.

Source: *Transportation in America,* Association of American Railroads, Washington, D. C., 1947, p. 17.

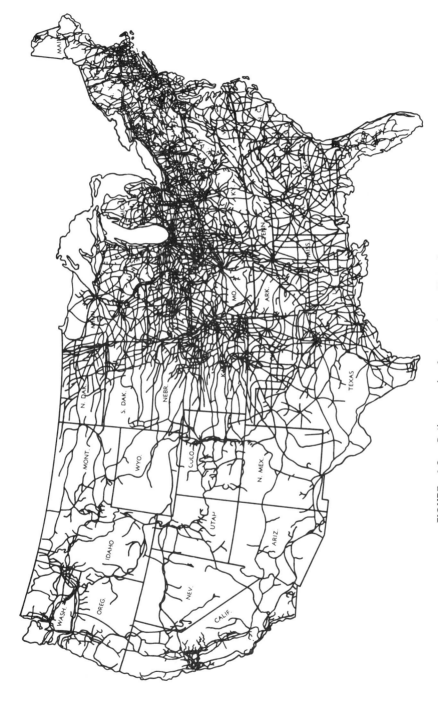

FIGURE. 4.2. Rail network of coterminous United States, 1966.

Source: *Railroads of America*, Association of American **Railroads**, Washington, D. C., April, 1966, p. 6.

3. Containers-on-Flatcar service (COFC)
4. Unit Trains
   a. Coal
   b. Grain
   c. Chemicals
   d. Potash
   e. Automobiles
   f. Trans-Continental
   g. Environmental Improvement
   h. Sectional
   i. Other potential kinds of unit trains
5. High-speed Passenger Trains

oversized cars

Freight cars of today are built to move 100 to 150 tons instead of the 40 to 50 tons which had been considered standard (and still are referred to as standard) from World War I days to the early 1960's. Many of the new, oversized cars have special loading/unloading aids which include flow hoppers, removable sides and tops, pumps, blowers, shakers, etc. Thus, not only do the larger cars reduce dead-hauling time but significantly reduce turnaround times.

The first oversized cars were 100-ton hoppers especially designed to move midwest grain into the Southeast.[1] Now the gamut of oversized cars includes flat, tank, hopper, gondola, box and rack cars.

TABLE 4.3
Coterminous United States Railroad Line Mileage *
Selected Years 1929-1968

Year	Line Mileage
1929	249,433
1939	235,064
1949	225,000 (est.)
1959	217,565
1964	212,603
1965	211,925
1966	211,107
1967	209,826
1968	209,000 (est.)

*The indicated mileage represents the aggregate length of roadway of all line-haul railroads. It does not include mileage of tracks in yards.
Source: *Yearbook of Railroad Facts* (1969 Edition, Association of American Railroads, Washington, D. C., April 1969), p. 60.

---

1. In the late 1940's A. L. Mechling barge lines and other water carriers began to barge grain from the midwest to Guntersville, Alabama, on the Tennessee. From Guntersville, the grain was trucked to poultry feeding areas in Georgia and northern Florida at transportation savings in excess of $1.00 per 100 lbs. The railroads' response to this form of competition was the Big John, a closed hopper car moving grain at low, competitive, multiple-car rates.

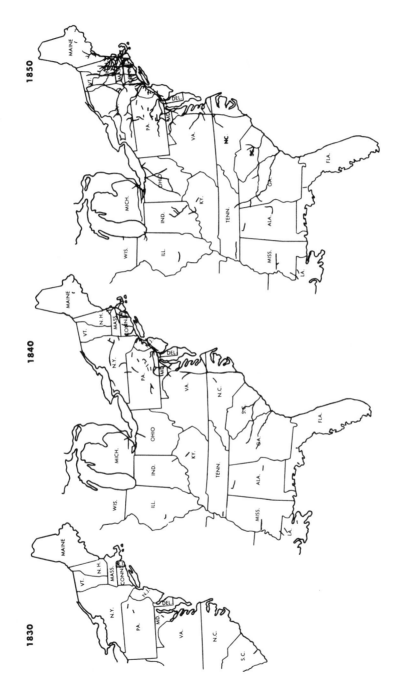

FIGURE 4.3. Early Patterns of United States Railroad network.

Source: *Railroads of America*, Association of American Railroads, Washington, D. C., April, 1966, p. 6.

31

TOFC

Trailer-on-Flatcar service includes many loading schemes; drive on-off (circus-train fashion) accounts for most of this kind of traffic. However, there are numerous other variations to include hoisting and side loading. There are also at least six different plans of service offered by the railroads and charged-for accordingly.[2]

Plan 1.   Railroad carriage of the trailers of motor common carriers.

Plan 2.   Railroad carriage of its own trailers, thus providing their own truck competitive service. Under Modified Plan 2, the customer pulls the trailer to and from the rail terminal and pays a somewhat lower rate than when the railroad performs this part of the service.

Plan 3.   Railroad carriage of shippers' trailers at a flat rate per mile.

Plan 4.   Railroad carriage of shippers' loaded or empty trailers on shippers' flatcars at a flat rate per car.

Plan 5.   Railroad carriage of their own or motor carrier trailers in coordinated service on joint rail-truck rate arrangement.

Plan 6.   Deals with the handling of less-than-truckload shipments in piggyback service.

That TOFC is a still growing success is evident in the data shown in Table 4.4. Much of the earlier growth took place in the 400-mile overnight shipment range radial to such rail transportation centers as Chicago, New York and Philadelphia. More recently, transcontinental hauls of trailers (to include refrigerator trailers) are accounting for an increasing share of TOFC freight.

COFC

Container-on-Flatcar is probably just now coming into its own. Currently this type of movement is only some 10 to 15 percent of the TOFC volume. It is very likely that an international standardization of containers will make the security and handling aspects of this service especially attractive on international and high-value shipments. It should be kept in mind that even though some of this business has been attracted to rail carriers from highway haulers, much of it is also freight that would probably have moved in boxcars.

unit trains

Moving a large number of identical (or near identical) cars as a unit promises to be one of the most significant technological developments in railroad history. Bulk commodities which flow are the prom-

---

2. P. T. McElhiney and C. L. Hilton, *Logistics and Traffic Management* (Wm. C. Brown Co. Publishers, Dubuque, Iowa, 1968), pp. 92-93.

ising commodities. The pattern of these commodities is shown in Figure 4.4. The savings range as much as 30 percent over other rail rate plans. Illustrative volumes for a single-unit train exceed 40,000 tons for coal; 1,800 automobiles; 15,000 tons for iron ore. In regard to coal and ores, hopper-loading techniques and either rotary or shaker unloading equipment speed turnaround times.

TABLE 4.4

TOFC Loadings

Year	United States	Eastern* District	Southern† District	Western‡ District
1955	168,150	n.a.	n.a.	n.a.
1956	207,783	102,646	1,617	103,520
1957	249,065	130,211	6,155	112,699
1958	278,071	139,070	8,903	130,098
1959	416,508	204,010	10,687	201,811
1960	554,115	263,817	21,128	269,170
1961	591,246	299,605	37,749	253,892
1962	706,441	369,840	64,783	271,818
1963	797,474	387,432	101,321	308,721
1964	890,748	434,039	122,529	334,180
1965	1,034,377	490,872	164,043	379,462
1966	1,162,731	539,213	193,055	430,463
1967	1,207,242	539,460	208,985	458,797
1968	1,337,149	589,092	236,756	511,301

*East of the Mississippi and North of the Ohio River (extended to Norfolk, Virginia.
†East of the Mississippi and South of the Ohio.
‡West of the Mississippi.
Source: *Yearbook of Railroad Facts* (Car Service Division, Association of American Railroads. 1969 Edition), p. 33.

Other potential markets for unit-train service include metropolitan environmental control (garbage hauling), transcontinental food shipments, agricultural machinery, limestone, plastics, through (in-load) international movements, and ores.

passenger service

With few exceptions, passenger service is fast disappearing. It is obvious that if and when passenger service again appears on the railroad rights-of-way that many changes will have been implemented. There is little doubt but that a demand exists for passenger service, especially for commuter and inter-city travel, up to distances of 400 ± miles. Whether the units will travel on rails or on elevated or tunneled tracks or other ways (not necesasrily steel rails) is conjectural at this time. The power used (turbine, electric, diesel, nuclear, etc.) will no doubt also be different, as will the levels of manpower requirements. It is

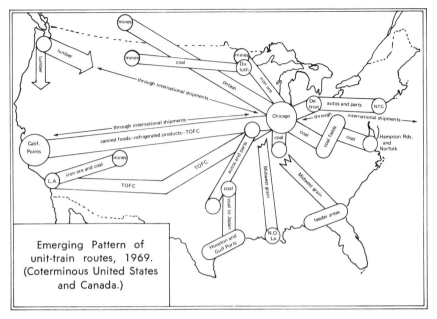

Emerging Pattern of
unit-train routes, 1969.
(Coterminous United States
and Canada.)

FIGURE 4.4.

clear that automation must be allowed to replace manpower and that
arrivals and departures must be programmed to meet demands.

In short, the current pattern of passenger traffic is that of a few
successful commuter runs such as are found radiating from Chicago
(especially west, south, and northwest) and New York. A few transcontinental trains are operating successfully but elsewhere most local rail
passenger service seems to have an extremely brief "half-life." Passenger
service, though soon to go, may well make an early return due to the
keen need to solve the nation's mass transportation problems.[3]

rails—an overview

Railroads form the basic framework of the nation's routeway pattern.
As railroads were developed across the country, lasting economic
changes occurred. Industries, markets and urbanization developed where
the rails served. Railroads truly serve as a national transportation system
between the mines, forests, farms and the ports on the one hand, and
the industrial, urban and rural markets on the other. As the only mode
of transport that has been in continuous existence (operation) since

---

3. The value of "famous-name" passenger trains in terms of advertisement value
remains undetermined as do problems dealing with "how-to-mass" the passenger
transportation market.

early industrialization, the railroads have more than any other carrier shaped the pattern of commodity flow throughout the nation.

The Basic Waterway Pattern

The earliest transport mode to be developed in the United States was the waterway. Rivers, lakes, and coastwise traffic were all developed early. So important a role has water and water traffic played in this nation's economic development that some 75 percent of the nation's population lives in communities located either on the coasts or on navigable rivers, canals, or lakes. Because of many basic differences it is best to discuss domestic waterway patterns separately from international deep-sea water-borne patterns.

Domestic Waterways

Domestic waterways, in turn, differ greatly in their type of operations among the shallow-draft barge industries, Great Lakes operations, and Coastwise Shipping.

Barge Industries

Within the United States there are some 28,500 miles of navigable streams and rivers with sufficient depth to float barges and/or towboats having drafts of six feet or more (See Figure 4.5). For the most part the shallow-draft barge industry operates at depths of nine feet or more. Their service provides chiefly for the movement of bulky commodities in barge-load quantities from 300 to 3,000 tons per barge. Indicative of the bulky nature of these commodities are the top 12 in terms of net tons moved (Table 4.5).

The top 12 commodities, in terms of volume, account for over 85 percent of all tonnages moved on the inland waterways. These data serve to emphasize the limited number and bulky nature of materials moved by inland water. As the figures indicate, coal, sand and gravel, petroleum and petroleum products, and grain and soybeans account for the preponderance of this traffic. And, in this connection, the *basic* nature of these commodities to the *basic* industries of the United States means that any savings in rates or resources developed because of the presence of waterway navigation are broadly based, population-wise.

The favorable orientation of the nation's major water courses to mineral deposits required by industries, especially the chemical industry, is shown on Figure 4.6. In addition to the materials indicated in Table 4.5, barge commodities include raw materials drawn from forests, agriculture, and sea water; if ports are recognized as a real source of

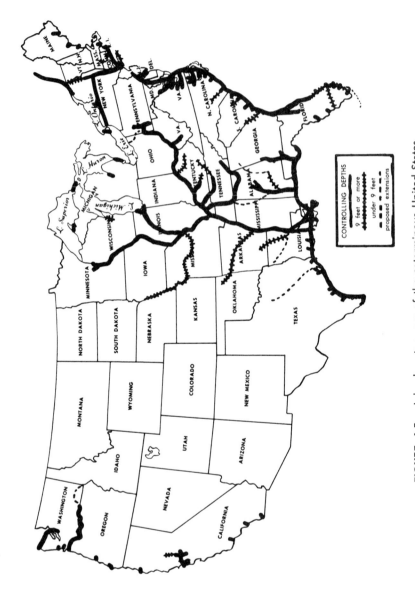

FIGURE 4.5. Inland waterways of the coterminous United States.

Source: *Big Load Afloat,* The American Waterways Operators, Inc., Washington, D. C., pp. 66-67

TABLE 4.5

Top Twelve Commodities Moved on the Inland Waterways of The United States, 1967 (Exclusive of The Great Lakes)

Commodity	Net Tons of 2000 Pounds
1. Bituminous Coal and Lignite	115,570,662
2. Petroleum and Kindred Coal Products	71,764,673
3. Sand and Gravel	58,650,911
4. Crude Petroleum	50,677,470
5. Gasoline	39,802,485
6. Marine shells, unmanufactured	23,362,780
7. Grain, grain products and Soybeans	22,117,013
8. Rafted logs	18,290,048
9. Basic chemicals and chemicals	7,444,821
10. Jet fuel	6,681,763
11. Iron and steel products	5,897,343
12. Sulphur	5,601,151
Total, Chief 12 commodities	425,861,120
All other commodities	75,051,513
Grand Total	500,912,513

Source: *1967 Inland Waterborne Commerce Statistics* (The American Waterways Operators, Inc., Washington, D. C., April 1969), p. 5.

imported raw materials than the relative orientation of these rivers and canals in respect to chemical development is even more favorable.

Availability of Adequate Plant Sites

The specific location and selection of industrial sites in general, and especially chemical plant sites, depends on: (1) adequate water supplies; (2) a large, nearly level, tract of land; (3) availability of low-cost electricity; and (4) an adequate supply of labor. Water requirements in chemical plants may run as high as 550,000 gallons per minute. Plants using 50,000 gallons of water per minute are common. Even this last figure equals the flow of streams usually considered rivers so that riparian sites on major waterways, or large lakes, are necessary to insure an adequate water supply for their operations.

Water requirements fall into three categories: (1) coolant; (2) plant processes; and (3) disposal medium for aqueous wastes. Although river water is used for all three, water used in most plant processes must be within a certain temperature range or degree of purity. Deep wells in alluvial bottom lands are usually depended upon to meet such requirements. There are literally hundreds of miles along the water routes containing sites with adequate ground-water supplies awaiting future development. Ground and surface water resources are still especially abundant along the Upper Mississippi and Tennessee Valleys and in

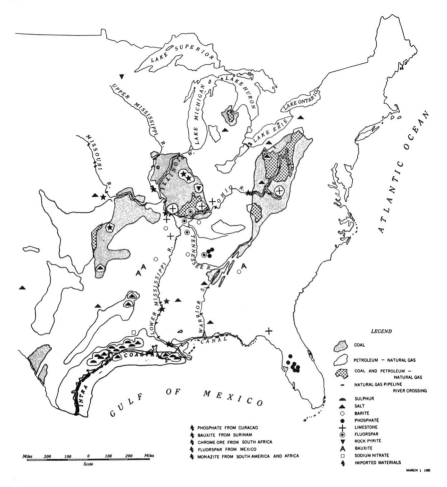

FIGURE. 4.6. Orientation of midwestern river and intra-coastal canal routes to raw materials consumed in chemical production.

the Lake and Bayou areas of Louisiana. Some Upper Mississippi cities have undeveloped resources of water of even temperature from sands and sandstones estimated to be in excess of 7,500,000 gallons per 24-hour day.[4]

Usually, chemical plants occupy large tracts of level land (a slope of 5 percent is considered to be about a maximum) where clusters of interdependent plants are situated: areas of 5,000 acres or even larger, may be needed. Here again, Midwestern Rivers and Canals traversing level glacial till plains, mature river bottoms, or recently emerged coastal

---

4. i.e., Along the Wisconsin River.

plains provide hundreds of miles of nearly ideal riparian sites. Only along some sections of the Ohio and Tennesseee Rivers do steep valleys hinder the siting of chemical plants. Nearly everywhere along the waterways, drainage and/or flood control projects assure dry sites.

Electric rates along the waterways are usually low because of the availability of coal by barge and/or hydropower.

Advantages of Transportation

Keen competition also forces chemical processors to pay close attention to economies in transportation. First of all, few chemical plants can be successful without a rail siding. As new trackage costs in the neighborhood of $80,000 per mile, the fact that the area traversed by the water routes is also served by some of the best and densest rail nets in an especially important advantage. Similarly, the value of good roads and road nets in the area cannot be overemphasized.

Every major petroleum or natural gas pipeline east of the Rockies either crosses these water routes or terminates at their banks. The significance of this is evident in the huge petro-chemical plants at Wood River, Illinois, and by the fact that at every point at which trunk natural gas pipelines cross the water routes there are chemical plants: for the most part these are plants producing either anhydrous ammonia or carbon black.

Furthermore, markets, processing sites, and raw materials along the Midwestern River and Intra-Coastal Routes are linked by a highly developed, low-cost, mass-in-bulk transportation system. Waterway carriers and shippers possess a wide range of equipment to move acids and other commodities on a scale to meet the demands of the endless belt and pipeline techniques used in modern chemical plants. Some newer barges have a capicity of 16,000 barrels, or the equivalent of nearly 70 railroad tank cars. There are acid barges with rubber-lined tanks; insulated hot caustic soda equipment; pressure units for the transporting of chlorine and propane or butane; stainless steel-lined alcohol barges; sulphur dome to processing plant sulphur barges; and, special styrene units. Nearly all equipment designed to move liquid chemicals is self-discharging. Endless belts, pneumatic tubes, or huge clam buckets load and unload non-liquid materials.

High-speed towing service considerably reduces the amount of capital tied up with in-transit materials. Also, equipment designed for use on either Gulf, River, Canal, or Great Lakes eliminates the necessity for transshipment breaks. This latter promises to be of special significance to Florida's phosphate industry which has major markets in the Midwest and Middle South. However, phosphates, sulphur, and other shipments are economically transshipped from barges to many inland points.

The Great Lakes and St. Lawrence seaways

In contrast with river and canal traffic, which as has been pointed out was dormant by 1895-97, traffic on the Great Lakes has, in general, continued to grow. By 1889 it amounted to 25,267,000 tons (net tons of 2000 pounds), by 1910 it was a most impressive 85,000,000 tons.[5] Today some 165,000,000 net tons move annually over the Great Lakes.[6]

The significance of the Great Lakes route is due chiefly to the location of iron ore, limestone, timber, grain, coal, and petroleum products surrounding the Lakes and to the heavy population centers which have evolved on the shores of the Lakes. Historically, the greatest iron ore deposits have been located west and south of Lake Superior, while one of the world's largest coal producing and iron/steel markets lies south, east, and west of Lakes Michigan, Huron, and Erie.

Since the opening of the Sag Channel, which connects Lake Calumet (and, in turn, Lake Michigan) with the Illinois Waterway(and, again in turn, the entire Mississippi Basin rivers and canals) and the opening of the St. Lawrence Seaway in 1959 with its 27-foot channel, the Great Lakes have become nationwide in their impact on domestic routeways and international in that ships of the world now ply these fresh waters.

inland waterways—an overview

Inland Waterways in the United States move approximately 10 percent of domestic trade over some 29,000 miles of channelized routes. The average cost to shippers is low (3 mills per ton mile on the average; 1.8 mills on the Intra-coastal and Lower Mississippi Rivers to 6 mills on some of the more difficult rivers to navigate, such as the Missouri).[7] Because industry (and people) need water for purposes other than navigation most of the nation's markets are festooned along the longer, and in most cases navigable, waterways; the rivers and canals, too, traverse areas rich in the production of basic, bulky commodities: coal, sand and gravel, petroleum (and petroleum products) and forest commodities.

In addition, the Great Lakes provide more than 1800 miles of the world's busiest water routes. These lakes serve to combine iron ore, coal, limestone, grain and petroleum products in the nation's industrial heartland and to receive and ship machines, tools, and other products worldwide.

---

5. E. L. Bogart, *Economic History of The American People* (Longmans, Green and Co. Ltd., New York, 1935), p. 641.

6. Based on 1966 data as reported in *1967 Inland Waterborne Commerce Statistics* (The American Waterways Operators, Inc., Washington, D. C., 1969), p. 6.

7. Rail costs to shippers is estimated at 14 mills per ton mile, trucks approximately 60 mills, and air freight at 180 mills per ton mile (although the latter may well tumble when, or if, the C5A-type aircraft becomes operational).

Foreign-Oriented Deep-Water Routes

The pattern of United States foreign ocean-trade routes is a combination of ports, port hinterlands, foreign origins or destinations, shapes of land masses, and the locations of major canals. Ocean traffic has to move through ports with the appropriate facilities for loading and unloading operations. Where natural harbors do not exist, man devises means to modify port geography to a degree needed to serve its hinterland. In regard to the existing foreign ocean trade routes, few man-made features have had greater impact than the Suez and Panama Canals (See Figure 1.2). The Panama Canal affected domestic traffic patterns as well. The opening of the west coast of South America to East Coast and Midwest industries affected domestic traffic to the West Coast and, too, the Panama Canal has affected domestic rate patterns.[8] Ships still follow routes which take advantage of currents, winds, and refueling points.

Most of the world's ocean traffic moves on five major ocean routeways (See Figure 1.2). These routeways are:

1. The North Atlantic Routeway
2. The North Pacific Routeway
3. The South African Routeway
4. The South American Routeway
5. The South Pacific Routeway

The high degree of service availability along these routeways includes frequency of vessel sailings, kinds of vessels, and such port facilities as docks, shipyards, and commercial facilities.[9]

The pattern of chief commodity exports and imports varies from routeway to routeway. These are better itemized than generalized and are shown detailed and discussed in *Essential United States Foreign Trade Routes,* a document published by the Maritime Administration, U. S. Department of Commerce, May, 1957.

In addition to the 33 essential United States foreign trade routes discussed in the publication referred to, the nation has three other categories of ocean movements: (1) Coastal; (2) Intercoastal, and (3) The 49th and 50th states, and territories. General cargo ships and commodity movements dominate trade to and from the latter and intercoastal with service usually provided by common carriers. Tankers and coal-hauling vessels dominate coastwise movements, especially the east coast traffic.

---

8. For example, some of the historical bases of "water compelled rates" to West Coast ports from eastern cities still account for certain rates from New York to San Francisco being lower than on the same shipment to Salt Lake City.

9. Banks, brokers, forwarders, marine insurers, sales representatives, foreign trade zones, entrepôt activities, etc.

Added to these generalizations are certain specialized cargo movements. To illustrate, wine moves from southern California ports to Corpus Christi, Texas, and the same vessel moves sugar and starches on the back haul. Logs are rafted along the west coast. Most of the traffic is bound from the west coast to Gulf and east coast ports and consists of lumber, canned foods, ores, and wheat. That it is difficult to obtain return hauls to the west coast is evident in the fact that scrap metal and oil are moved. To a large degree these movements can be likened to carrying coal to Newcastle.

Much of the coastwise traffic is intra-corporate in nature rather than between firms. That is, as long as volume materials are *within* a firm's own pipeline, lowest possible costs are usually sought; when movements *between* firms occurs, there are often other considerations of time, warehousing costs, or terminal facilities that can be over-riding. (See Figure 4.7).[10]

Merchant Marine Act of 1936

Due to prevailing higher wage rates, higher operating costs, safety standards, and corresponding higher construction costs the Merchant Marine Act of 1936 makes available subsidies for the construction, maintenance, and operation of ships under United States registry. Even so, most U S firms operating vessels in international trade find it more economical to place thir ships under a foreign flag, thus avoiding rules and regulations governing crew size, wages, and certain other safety measures such as having to furnish a medical officer if more than 12 passengers are carried and what are considered an excessive and costly number of safety inspections and installations. Panama and Liberia registries are particularly popular. Thus, for example, these two countries literally haul much of the commerce of the United States and show deep-sea tonnages far in excess of their own national needs.

deep-sea traffic—an overview

Deep-sea traffic should be seen as but extensions of the domestic routeways (See Figure 1.1). Meeting in the nation's ports, the deep-sea routes (Figure 1.2) reach out to bring the world's goods to the nation's ports, which for purposes of understanding domestic patterns are but domestic origins of these commodities from overseas. In terms of the number and kinds of vessels, it would appear that the United States merchant fleet is far too small for a nation of such great economic activity, but to this total must be added millions of tons of shipping

---

10. Dow Chemical's operation of their own vessels between their plants located on the Gulf and Atlantic coast typifies this practice.

FIGURE 4.7. Marine Dow-Chem ports of call.

Source: Dow Chemical Corporation, Freeport, Texas.

under the commercial or economic control of U S firms, even though these ships may be of foreign registry.

The Highway Pattern

introduction

The pattern of modern roads in the United States began in the same economic growth era (1890-1918) that spawned an interest in transport forms other than railroad. Due to the growth of cities, urban sprawl was already in evidence; railroads, too, were looking for better roads over which to move shipments to their terminals. Then, too, bicycle and carriage manufacturers were anxious to see better roads and the still preponderance of population on the farms were looking for ever better and more reliable farm to market roads. For the most part, however, roads were primarily seen as feeders to the rail system.

With Ford's mass-produced Model T (1909) highway planning, construction and maintenance, which had been a local government (village, city, township and county) responsibility, now came under the aegis of State and Federal governments (Federal Aid Road Act, 1916). Today for the first time in the history of the United States a nationwide highway development program is underway. Heretofore, highway programs from the nationwide point-of-view had been segmented, relatively unplanned; implemented piecemeal by the various levels of state, county, and urban governments in response to a whole host of pressures, local, state, or federal. The impact of the new federal highway program on industry, even though built in conformation with the nation's basic routeway pattern (See Figures 1.1 and 4.8), especially industrial location, promises to stagger the imaginations of even the most visionary of our top-level industrial managers.

Enough of the new highway system has now been completed to serve as an indicator of things to come for U S transport. What responses have our industries made to these new roads and prospects of future extensions? What impact have these new roads had on industry? What impact will they have in the future?

These questions are discussed below.

FIGURE 4.8. Proposed pattern of federal interstate highways.

pattern of the new interstate system

By 1975 the National Interstate Highway System will consist of 41,000 miles of 2, 4, 6, 8, or even 10 lane freeways crisscrossing the country, moving traffic faster and more safely. By completion date these routes will serve nearly 85 percent of the urban population, 90 percent of the cities over 50,000, 42 of the state capitals, and will carry over one-fourth of the nation's traffic.

Almost by necessity the system will leave some important inequities. For example, Houston, Texas, badly needs better highway routes to the northeast (to St. Louis, Chicago, Memphis, and Little Rock) and there is a real need for a route southwestward along the Gulf. Understandably there are other areas similarly restricted. Fort Worth wants a route to the northwest. Norfolk, Virginia, and the eastern shore desire a coastal route along the Atlantic Coast. Little Rock is restricted to east-west traffic as are Tulsa, Bismarck, Charleston, and many other cities. However, the basis of routes designated included (supposedly) considerations of traffic densities and military requirements as well as geographical patterns.

industrial development along the new interstate roads

That modern thruways have a favorable economic influence on the belt traversed is evident from the degree of industrial development that has been aligned adjacent to them. No simple before and after comparisons are possible because of the great number of variables involved. However, the sheer number of plants located on turnpikes, freeways, and other intrastate-type highways in contrast to other roads and streets argues strongly for their continued importance as industrial location factors.

Illustrating the power of expressways as an industrial location force are the reports from some of the early projects. For example, between June 1955 and September 1958 the number of industrial firms along Massachusetts Route 128 (the Boston Loop) increased from 39, with 14 under construction, to 209 in operation and 17 more under construction. Today there are over 270 such plants and more under construction, an increase more than four-times as great as for any other section of the entire state of Massachusetts. Elsewhere on the East Coast similar results can be noted; for example, over $300 million has been invested in new plants along the New York Thruway. The Shirley Highway, leading southwest out of Washington, D. C., has not only become the axis of over 350,000 people but has also played the key role in the development of the Shirley Industrial District. On the West Coast the story is similar in that almost 50 percent of the dollars invested in Alameda County, California, was for plants sited along the Eastshore

Freeway. In Chicago, industrial locations at points readily accessible to the Tri-State Highway have been established at a rate four to five times that for the rest of the metropolitan area.

locational advantages to industry

The reasons for industry moving to the new Interstate routes are many, some obvious, others extremely subtle; all difficult to measure accurately in terms of dollars and cents. In general, however, they fall into seven major categories: (1) freight transportation savings; (2) access to wider markets; (3) access to satellite and ancillary plants; (4) employee relations; (5) dispersion; (6) advertising; and (7) economic stimulations.

Freight transportation savings are realized in several areas. First of all, operators on the New York Thruway have found it feasible to reduce the horsepower of road tractors from 200 to 175 horsepower; thus saving from $1200 to $1500 per unit, not to mention some 3000 pounds in weight. This lowering of horsepower requirements results not only from reducing grades but also from reducing starts and stops. For example, Indiana's tollroad, as compared with the much worked-on parallel U S 20, eliminates 78 stop lights, 18 railroad crossings, 1 drawbridge, 15 school zones, and 20 major highway intersections. Freight savings are too lengthy to discuss in detail here. Perhaps they are best summarized under the following headings:

1. Reduction of time (maximum utilization of vehicles, wages, and better satisfied customers).
2. Savings in fuel cost (by reducing the requirement in tractive effort).
3. Savings in equipment costs, (lower initial costs, longer life of brakes, clutches, and tires).
4. Savings through safety (lower insurance and economy of human element, not to mention humanitarian aspects).

The second reason given for industry's move to the Interstate Highway, access to wider markets, may be easily recognized; the importance of this factor is not so evident. To illustrate, a glass boat manufacturer was in the process of locating a new plant in Norfolk, Virginia, when the accompanying map (See Figure 4.9) was called to his attention. The map indicates the logical truck-trailer delivered market from a Norfolk site, and around this, the market area that could be reached at comparable costs (with comparable equipment) by simply locating the proposed plant at Petersburg on an Interstate Highway. A decision to locate at Petersburg was implemented.

The third factor attracting industry to the new highway system, access to satellite and ancillary plants, is well illustrated by the example set by the General Electric Company with their Syracuse, Buffalo, Auburn, Utica, and Schenectady plant complex oriented along the New York Thruway with headquarters at Electronics Park, Syracuse.

The fourth industrial attraction afforded by the Interstate Highway covers employee relations. Recruitment of labor from a wider area is possible with thruway development. A plant two minutes from a thruway, for instance, can attract workers from 15 to 20 miles away, and it takes them no longer to get to their jobs than if they lived five miles away from a plant in the same city. Thus, workers can have a wider choice of living situations. Both serve to give plant locators a freer hand in plant dispersion.

This dispersion factor, for many plants, is limited to a degree by a real need for complementary rail facilities. Hence, many firms need-

FIGURE 4.9. Comparison of delivered market accessibility for small boats, Norfolk versus Petersburg.

ing both must locate accordingly in spite of the fact that plant sites at Interstate Highway points where these routes are paralleled or crossed by rail facilities are relatively limited and costly.

The fifth factor is the increased dispersion encouraged by the new highway, not only for better living but for military considerations as well, especially in this day when two plants even 15 miles apart constitute one target.

The sixth economic advantage may be said to be the accompanying advertising benefits. This is an advantage on which it is next to impossible to place a price; but an attractive, impressive structure, located in full view of literally hundreds of thousands of people, is bound to have a salutary impact.

That economic stimulation accompanies freeway construction cannot be denied. Engineering contractors and suppliers of building materials, earth-moving equipment, and the like will enjoy a lively business not only during the construction period but in the maintenance and upgrading that must necessarily follow.[11]

dislocations to industry

Can all of the above advantages to industry be obtained without cost to industry? Obviously the answer is no, but here again, even though the answer is obvious in terms of expected tax increments, some of the other dislocational factors inherent in such a highway program are not as obvious. There are three chief categories of these dislocational pressures on industry: (1) higher taxes, (2) depression of areas and industries non-contiguous to the new highways, and (3) skyrocketing land values.

The factor of higher taxes is well recognized. Citizens are already paying a per gallon tax plus other user taxes for these new highways and more increases appear certain if the routes are to be completed at any time even approaching the projected completion dates. As all industries cannot benefit equally from highway expenditures, it stands to reason that certain inequities are bound to result; hence the emphasis on user-type taxes for specific allocations to these projects.

Depression of areas and industries non-contiguous to the new highways is very real and growing in severity. To illustrate, the City Planning Department of the Massachusetts Institute of Technology reports

---

11. The U. S. Department of Public Roads reports that from 1960 to 1973 the following materials will be required for each million dollars spent: (1) 420 to 425 tons of iron and steel; (2) 1.4 billion barrels of cement; (3) 128 million tons of bituminous material; (4) 9.7 million tons of aggregate; (5) 13 billion gallons of petroleum products; (6) 1.8 billion tons of explosives; (7) 908,000 new traffic signs annually; (8) 5 million gallons of paint each year; (9) 443,000 highway workers (each of whom requires from three to four nonhighway workers in support).

that the town of Needham estimates that its tax rate would be held down by $10 per $1,000 during the next ten years. This not only penalizes the community but it also penalizes the community's industries through either higher taxes or less adequate services.

Investors in improved real estate also are feeling the pinch. In Dallas, Texas, an estimated two-thirds of the business establishments along the Central Expressway moved to these sites from other Dallas locations. Also, holders of improved land along new freeways will enjoy four, five, or even more times the opportunity to sell their property.

Industries *per se* are similarly affected. Many concerns whose competitors are now, or soon will be, situated on or close to an Interstate Route are less easily able to broaden their markets. In fact, many are in danger of losing their traditional markets to their more fortunate rivals. The impact of these developments may be especially severe on many concerns; for example, oil distributors whose profit is dependent on a fixed percentage of volumes handled.

The third major cost of these new highways to industry is higher land costs. For example, in Houston land values along the existing or planned freeways are usually 700 to 800 percent higher than noncontiguous areas. Indeed, where rail and intersection are especially favorable, they may be 5000 percent higher. These costs are so high that even for those firms dealing primarily with distribution problems, the payoff periods for Interstate Highway sites may run to 50 or 60 years.

Many concerns (and, indirectly, communities) are unable to finance such high-cost locations and are, therefore, either faced with a continuing operational handicap or with a costly move. The sum-total effect of these dislocation factors is to increase the cost of doing business with accompanying inflationary tendencies.

Highway Overview

Roads in the nation, other than Interstate Highways, have become feeder or supplementary routes local in nature or ancillary at best to the new limited access routes. Indeed, in many states, such as Illinois, the older routes have suffered from a lack of development or simple neglect in favor of Interstate Highway Development, further augmenting the concentration of markets, manufacturers and logistical facilities along the routeways and serving to further isolate, in a relative but real sense, as many, or even more, areas than are actually being served by the new roads. In any event, the new Interstate Highways have added strong augmentations to the attractions of the nation's major routeways.

Air Transportation Patterns

Modern, non-stop, air services for both passengers and freight makes possible direct contact between any two cities. Accordingly, to a degree, air transportation has erased certain of the major routeway concepts presented thus far. However, historically, it was only logical to establish service along the traditional trade routes. Limitations of early aircraft in terms of range and altitude forced that considerations be given to water-level routes, mountain passes, and the avoidance of routes which offered frequent fogs and storms. Thus, early flights were routed along railroad, highway and river valley routes. Airfields, navigational aids and market developments corresponded; all three combining to fix air routes along the major transportation corridors modified by certain point-to-point, non-stop routes between *major* air terminals of *major* cities already well established and dependent upon the services provided by *major* routeway facilities.

Today, the chief factors of the United States air routes are

1. Major Domestic Trunk Carriers
2. Feeder Routes
3. Overseas Carriers
4. Local, Metropolitan-Suburban Services
5. All-Freight Carriers
6. Military Air-Transportation Services

major domestic trunk carriers

The major domestic trunk carriers are those airlines having permanent operating rights[12] to operate high density trafic routes between the principal traffic generation centers of the United States. There are (as of this writing) 11 major domestic air carriers. These carriers are: American, Braniff International, Continental, Delta, Eastern, National, Northeast, Northwest, Trans World, United, and Western.

domestic overseas carriers

Overseas carriers include extensions of certain of the United States carriers to include: Braniff International, Eastern, National, Northwest, and Trans World.[13] In addition, Pan American Airways is an overseas United States carrier with its primary service areas overseas (See Figure 4.10).

---

12. Based on the issuance of certificates of convenience and necessity by the Civil Aeronautics Board (CAB). It can be revoked or modified by the same government agency contingent on needs, service levels, or abilities to perform.

13. Additional overseas operational rights, are under consideration for American, Continental, and United. Any final determination will no doubt be made in the highest court.

feeder routes

In the United States there are several classes of feeder routes. Many are major in the scope of their services, serving as much as one-fourth of the nation (Figs. 4.11-12). Others are extremely small and provide limited services in terms of equipment, schedules, and geographic areas transversed. To an increasing degree, so-called feeder routes are being authorized to fly from focal cities in their service areas to major metropolitan centers beyond what has been considered their primary service areas. The chief reason for granting extra-territorial routes to the feeder carriers is to reduce traffic through such congested air terminals as O'Hare Field, northwest of Chicago, Illinois.[14] Los Angeles, New York, Atlanta and Washington, present similar problems of heavy traffic.

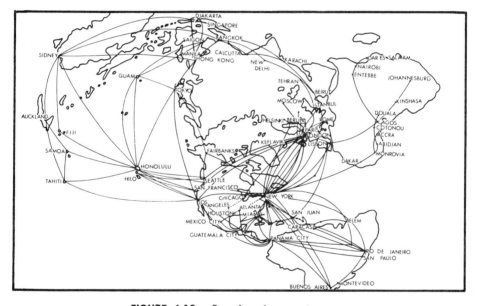

FIGURE 4.10. Pan American routeways.

overseas airlines

The termination of World War II, the Korean Campaigns, and (even before its termination) the Vietnam Effort have seen additional domestic airlines seeking overseas extension. Prior to World War II, the Pan

---

14. Illustrative of this development is the one and two-stop service inaugurated by Ozark Airlines from Peoria, Illinois, to Washington, D. C., and New York. This service began in early 1969 and now allows passengers to by-pass O'Hare Field with that airport's attendant time requirements and frequent delays due to congestion.

American World Airways System was dominant in terms of flying the American flag at overseas airports. However, extra wartime demands for reliable, in volume, air transport has produced additional experienced personnel, and requisite equipment, to successfully operate into foreign destinations.

In a series of overseas route applications in the years immediately following World War II, the Civil Aeronautics Board certified competition for Pan American Airways into almost every area served by

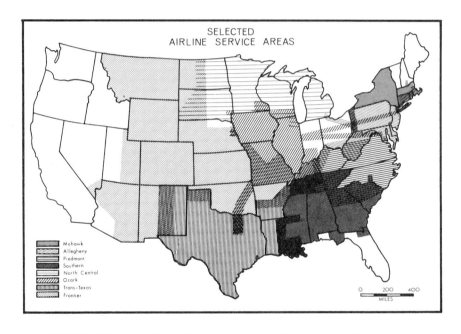

FIGURE 4.11. Overlap of selected regional airline service areas.

them. Braniff in South America; Trans-World to European and Asian points; United to Hawaii; Northwest to Asian destinations across the North Pacific (via Alaska, with Trans-World and Northwest meeting in India). Following the Korean conflict, Northwest received added authorizations in the Pacific Basin and now, even before the termination of hostilities in Vietnam, both American and Continental are receiving favorable consideration of requests to reach into the Far East and the Oceania-Australia areas.

Both of these airlines, especially Continental Airlines, are investing in hotel chains in order to develop destinations and ancillary facilities to attract customers into these areas of otherwise doubtful traffic levels as of 1969.[15]

Wherever United States carriers fly, reciprocal rights are given to airlines of the nations reached. Thus, for practical considerations, the pattern of overseas flights as they leave, or arrive, in the United States are through those major air terminals which offer sufficient traffic flows to warrant customs clearance procedures: New York, Chicago, Washington, D. C., (Dulles), Miami, Houston, Los Angeles, San Francisco, etc.

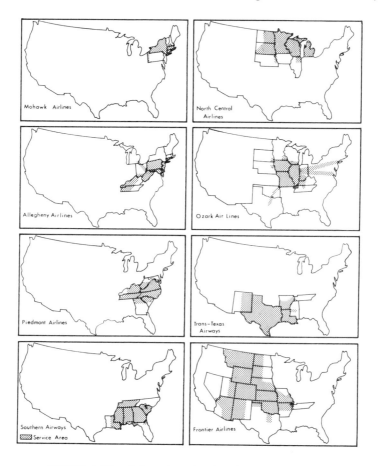

FIGURE 4.12. Selected regional airline service areas.

15. This pattern is receiving increasing attention and investments. Integration of transportation with resort and other tourist attractions and facilities is being promoted as a stimulus to travel and to broaden travel markets. See the section on "Total Travel Package" in the next chapter.

local metropolitan services

Local services between airports within and around major metropolitan areas is of increasing importance. The Pan American building in New York City has a helioport on its roof, as do numerous major office buildings in the nation's metropolitan centers. Helioports for both passengers and mail are part of accepted air traffic patterns at major air terminals (Figure 4.13).

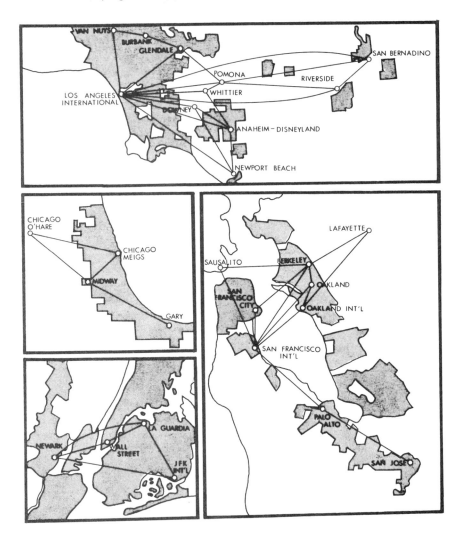

FIGURE 4.13. Local air service patterns of Los Angeles, Chicago, New York, San Francisco and Oakland.

Similarly, short feeder lines with small-sized equipment fly into smaller, more conveniently located airports such as Meigs Field on Chicago's lake front. These lines add to schedules and reach into areas which do not warrant the use of heavier, larger, aircraft in use by the major feeder or trunk air lines. These services are too numerous to detail but are sufficiently common as to have become integral parts of the nation's airline system. In every case, these services heighten the transport concentrated along the nation's major routeways.

all-freight air carriers

Today the all-freight carriers are moving freight to and from some 50-60 metropolitan centers which are focal to regional hubs and situated astride one of the nation's major routeways (Figure 4.14).[16] Now, and increasingly so, most of the country's 570 ± commercial airports are feeding into and out of these 50 to 60 JOCAMA CENTERS.[17] Inter-

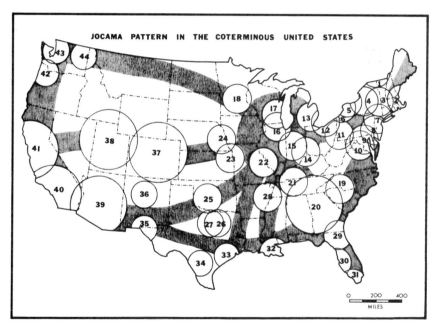

FIGURE 4.14. Relationship of major routeways to JOCAMA pattern in the coterminous United States.

Source: Based on "Distribution Management Tips," *Transportation and Distribution Management*, Vol. 8, No. 12, December, 1968.

16. Called JOCAMA, an acronym for Jet Operating Center and Marketing Area. See "Distribution Management Tips," *Transportation and Distribution Management*, December, 1968.
17. *Ibid.*

state and dense supporting highway nets serve industries and markets within a 200 ± radius of these focal points (See Figure 4.14). The cost of airport construction, and their predicted priorities below new highway expenditures, may well limit the number of cities which can reasonably be expected to have jet dimension fields at the expense of highways. This factor, combined with the reasoning that as jets become larger (and economics of scale favor the use of jumbo jets in the movement of air freight), fewer airports will be able to handle them. Fewer and fewer cities will be served by jumbo jets as air freight will move faster, by truck rather than between planes, only to have to eventually be loaded into a truck for ultimate delivery.

In 1968 air transportation moved approximately 70 percent of all intercity commercial passengers in the United States. Their share of freight movements remained at less than one percent by weight.[18] Continued growth is threatened more by the limited capacities of terminal facilities at such transportation hubs as New York, Chicago and Washington than by a lack of markets *per se*. Significantly, the regular domestic airlines haul more freight and mail than the all-freight carriers with some 80 percent of all intercity first class mail going by air.[19] Thus carriers are concerned with *both* passenger and freight markets.

military air-transportation services

The Military Air Transport Service routes are important movers of both personnel and freight. In addition, historically, MATS has been the pioneer of modern aircraft and navigation techniques which have proven that domestic and overseas long-range flights are feasible. MATS air route encompasses much of the world to include logistical support to maintain the nation's military and attaché posture. More and more, MATS operations are being contracted out to commercial carriers; in turn, this trend has helped in the extension of domestic carrier operations to and from overseas destinations.

an overview of air transportation patterns

Continued rapid progress in the size and speed of equipment and navigation techniques, combined with such factors as Interstate Highway developments, are resulting in the use of ever larger plane capacities, both passenger and freight. These factors, combined, are reinforcing similar factors in other carriers to develop corresponding economies of scale in terms of the markets to be reached (chiefly the densely populated, industrialized metropolitan strip cities) and the volumes of

---

18. *Air Transport Technology, Handling and Shipping,* January, 1969, p. 52.
19. *Ibid.*

passengers and freight to be moved, to cause greater and greater con-
centrations of transportation activities and facilities at modal points
along the nation's major routeways.

Pipeline Transportation Patterns

Pipelines, the silent carriers, have arrived as one of the nation's
important transporters of bulk commodities. Today there are four main
categories of pipelines movements (other than water): (1) petroleum,
to include both crude oil and petroleum products; (2) natural gas; (3)
anhydrous ammonia; and (4) slurried commodities. A fifth type to
transport dry bulk commodities in capsules is under consideration and
study. Pipeline transportation now moves nearly 20 percent of all intercity freight as measured in ton miles.[20]

crude oil pipeline patterns

The pattern of crude oil pipelines consists of gathering lines and
trunk lines to refineries or ports (inland and ocean ports). The crude
oil gathering lines collect petroleum from wells and move it to oil
field tanks. Chemical analyses at these tanks determine how and when
the crude is to be fed into trunk lines for movement to refineries or
ports. Following the separation of crude at refineries or chemical plants
into products, the different refined products are blocked into trunk
product lines for movement to bulk storage or distribution tanks.

The general pattern of crude oil pipeline movements in the 48
coterminous states is shown on Figure 4.15. The movement of crude
from the producing fields to points along the routeways (Figure 1.1)
is evident. Initially, pipeline construction was concentrated in the producing fields and between the producing fields and refinery, chemical
plants, or ports. During the past decade this pattern has shifted to an
emphasis on refined-product lines.

refined petroleum product lines

Automation, remote computerized controls, large diameter pipelines,
and an almost complete dependence on electric power rather than diesel
are the distinctive facets of modern product lines. Typical of the new
era in product lines are the 600-mile, 36-inch, Colonial Pipeline from
Houston (Gulf Coast) to the Greater New York markets and an even
larger diameter, 40-inch, 600-mile line from the Gulf Coast to Greater
Chicago market areas. The economies of larger pipelines with less fric-

---

20. *Pipeline Transportation, Handling and Shipping,* January 1968, p. 84,
states that pipelines now account for nearly 17 per cent of the nation's total intercity
freight, as measured in ton miles (1967 data).

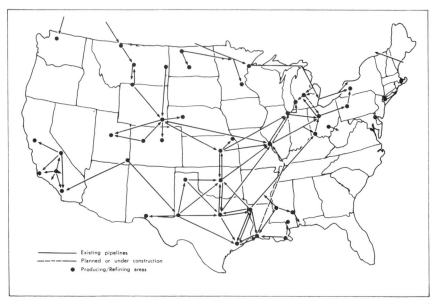

FIGURE 4.15.   Orientation of crude oil pipelines in the United States.

Source: "A State-of-the-Art Report from TAA," *Handling and Shipping*, January, 1968, p. 19.

tion per volume, and better use of pumping facilities have effected significant per-ton-mile cost reductions so that costs are now lower than 3 mills per ton-mile,[21] which approaches water transport rates. To attain these economies not only are new lines being built, but older lines are being rebuilt.

The pattern of petroleum product pipelines is shown on Figure 4.16. Most of these movements from refinery to market serve to move products to routeway market areas (Figure 1.1). Micro-wave tower communication systems are integral to the pipeline systems and serve to open valves (gates) governing the entrance or exit of given products in a product line. Thus, numerous different products can be moved through a given line and the service levels of a common carrier are being realized. Attendant controls and regulations are facing the industry. Offsetting these, of course, would be a degree of market security and certain legal aids in applying rights-of-eminent domain procedures.[22]

natural gas pipelines

Natural gas pipelines connect gas fields with markets. Distributors, with the exception of relatively few major industrial users, take gas from

21. *Op. cit.*, p. 84.
22. "A-State-of-the-Art Report from TAA," *Handling and Shipping* (January, 1968), p. 18.

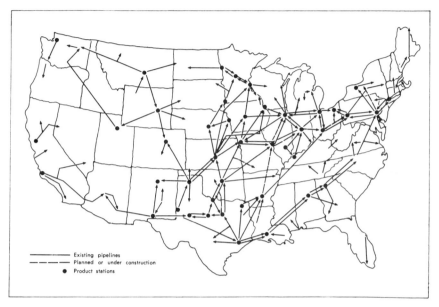

FIGURE 4.16. Orientation of product pipelines in the United States.
Source: "A State-of-the-Art Report from TAA," *Handling and Shipping*, January, 1968, p. 18.

the trunk pipelines and deliver it to the myriad-ultimate consumer. In the case of natural gas, to a disproportionate degree, resource development has awaited the transportation medium. Technology had first to reach a level in which large-diameter, seamless pipe could be developed. As house-space heating is the primary use of piped natural gas, capacities must be built to accommodate the peak use periods, namely, winter months. Thus, to create an off-season market, the natural gas applies interruptable rates to large industrial users. Also, as with the tank farms of the petroleum pipeline companies, storage areas for natural gas form an important part of the system: sealed mine cavities, worked-out gas and petroleum fields, and steel tanks are used to assure reservoirs of gas in the market areas.

The pattern of natural gas pipelines and gas fields is shown on Figure 4.17. Here, again, the ancillary nature of these transportation facilities to the nation's major routeways are in evidence. The fact that the natural gas pipeline companies connect producing fields to their markets, striplike in their geographic shapes and oriented along the routeways, means that the operators of these pipelines are regulated by availability and price of gas, on the one hand, and on the interest in gas as a fuel or energizer in the marketplace. Thus, this type of pipeline transportation is similar to other transportation media except that interstate hauls come under the jurisdiction of the Federal Power Com-

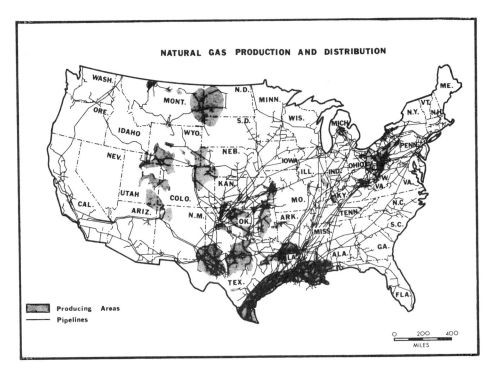

FIGURE 4.17. Natural Gas production and distribution. (Based on data provided by the Natural Gas Association.)

mission[23] rather than the Interstate Commerce Commission, Federal Aviation Administration, or Civil Aeronautics Board.

anhydrous ammonia pipelines

A pipeline designed and constructed to move anhydrous ammonia from Gulf Coast plants to rural markets in Iowa and surrounding states is ready to operate. The impact of this pipeline movement on rail tank movements will be severe. Similar attempts to move other fertilizer and limestone by pipeline in the forseeable future seems assured. Admittedly, this particular direction from industrial areas to rural areas off the major routeways is counter to most transportation developments underway or contemplated. But, in turn, higher agricultural yields will eventually move to the metropolitan market areas and this movement will, by necessity, augment the nation's over-riding transportation routeway patterns.

---

23. Natural Gas Act of 1938.

slurry pipelines

For those commodities which are chemically stable and capable of being mixed with water or some other liquid at a nominal cost for crushing and mixing at the point of loading, and dried and reprocessed at the destination, slurry pipeline offers the advantages of a uniform delivery rate and quality. This type of movement offers further advantages of economy where land and other right-of-way costs are high, where terrain may be rugged or combined with water obstacles, or where winter climates are severe. Although it has not been determined whether or not slurry lines are indeed competitive with unit train rates, the fact that the operation of such lines is under consideration and study cannot but have a salutory effect on freight rates, at least from the shipper's point-of-view. Coal has been moved as a slurry in a pipeline. Other potential slurry pipeline commodities are wood chips, iron ores, sulphur, limestone, and wet grain to be used in producing industrial alcohols. Other possibilities exist, and for those cases in which unstable dry-bulk solids might be involved, capsule pipelines are being considered.

capsule pipelines

Giving emphasis to the dynamic nature of pipeline transport patterns is the research and development work underway.[24] Some of the commodities being considered for this form of transport are those commodities which might have to be placed in capsules, canisters, or soft plastic bags; still other commodities might be prepared as paste slugs. In many cases, existing operating petroleum pipelines might be used to move such products. If capsule transport techniques prove feasible, the impact on existing modes might well be of sufficient scope to modify many present operational patterns. Possible limitations are the cost of loading, unloading, and handling capsules; backhaul costs if capsules are not usable or disposable; fixed (limited) rights-of-way or route; and propellant selection. In some cases the already high capital costs requisite to pipeline construction might well have to be increased to provide return lines for capsules or canisters.

an overview of pipelines transportation patterns

Continuing technological advancements have created a dynamic state of flux in the pipelines industries. Dramatic accomplishments in the automation of pipeline loadings/unloadings and control and increased pipe diameters have effected lowered shipping costs so that pipeline transportation offers real economies to shippers and ultimate consumers alike. And there are many prospects for commodities by pipeline, to

24. *Op. cit.*, p. 87. The "A Solids Pipeline R & D Association" is undertaking a $4.75 million program.

include different kinds and qualities of crude oil, petroleum products, natural gas, stable slurry, adaptable commodities, or unstable dry-bulk commodities. The sheer variety and orientation of such commodities moving from production areas to markets suggests that both reinforcement of existing routeways and distribution to rural areas from industries along the routeways will take place.

Special or Limited Carrier Patterns

Conveyor belts, pneumatic tubes, aerial tramways, air cushion machines, and electric interurban lines have many forms or variations. Although of local importance, these transport forms usually are used to supplement the major routeways. For example, aerial tramways or buckets are used to move bauxite from mines to docks in Jamaica; both pneumatic tubes and covered conveyor belts are used to deliver cement to riparian silos located along the Illinois and other waterways for loading into barges. Wherever special or limited carriers are used they are, in effect, supplemental to the major routeways.

The Carriers and the Major Routeways

To function effectively in terms of transportation markets to be served, carriers find it best in terms of operational costs and profit margins to move between metropolitan-industrial centers strung along a route. When several carriers compete along a route, a routeway evolves. Through attempts to generate traffic, carriers serve to reinforce the routeways by adding still more advantages to those already in effect along such transport arteries. Numerous other advantages exist so that along these routes are to be found the chief cybernations of a logistics system now providing the transportation services of the country.

Chapter 5

Cybernetics and Business Logistics and Their Geographic Patterns

Cybernetics can be defined as the science of basic data, communication of feedback, and control(s). The science, in application, can be (and probably is) used in almost all, indeed if not all, decision-making situations. Essentially, cybernetics deals with the dynamics of an entire system, including its sub-systems and the controls which limit or affect the functions of that system.

In this regard, business logistics includes both shipper and carrier transportation and accompanying communications systems. These operate through regional arteries of rail, highway, air, water, pipeline, or other transport mode. Especially do the accompanying communications systems offer maximum opportunities for capitalizing on the cybernetics concept.

The Relationship of the Cybernetics Concept to Business Logistics

Cybernetics deals with the entirety or wholeness of a dynamic system and the application of *cybernetics* depends on "systems thinking" or use of a systems approach. Basic to an understanding of how cybernetics underlies and undergirds *business logistics* is an appreciation of the fact that business logistics are inherently regional or interregional, at least in terms of having boundaries. Where do routes and routeways lead? Where do they terminate? What kind of commodities or traffic are carried on these routes or routeways? At what costs? For what purposes? In brief, the parameters of transportation (and hence business logistics) are regional in character (Figure 5.1).

Regional-interregional views of business logistics is (near) macro even though it deals specifically with the ebb and flow of shipments between regions. Thus, the concept is based on geography first and then on institutions and functions as these operate within, through and

INTER-REGIONAL AND REGIONAL PATTERNS
OF
BUSINESS LOGISTICS
A.
INTER-REGIONAL PATTERN

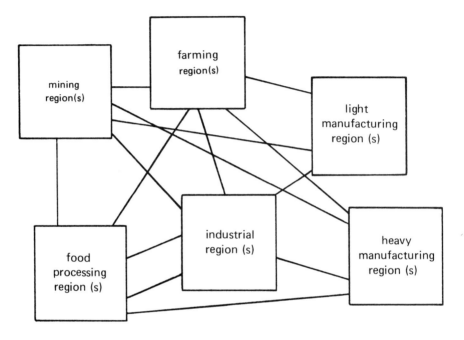

B.
REGIONAL (INPUT/OUTPUT) PATTERN

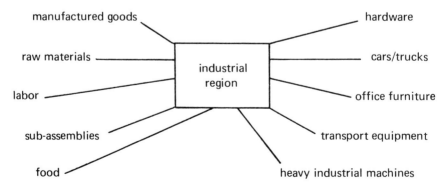

FIGURE 5.1.   Inter-regional/regional patterns of business logistics.

on regional frameworks. One way to look at business logistics problems is to consider the reasons behind the ebb and flow of materials between the different producing and consuming regions of the nation.

A second level approach is possible through a study of cybernetics. What are the signals that trigger the movements of goods and materials between regions? Thus, this second level approach necessarily builds upon the findings of the first approach.

The ebb and flow of goods and materials may be considered in terms of "Commodity Flows" between regions[1] or "Input/Output Studies of Regions" (compare Figure 5.1A with Figure 5.1B). In terms of business logistics, a region is usually both a producer and consumer, thus it also functions as a market in that goods and materials are concentrated, stored, sorted, assorted, disseminated and transported.

In regard to regions, for nearly 3500 years geographers have been attempting to understand the wholeness of regions. To date these students of geography have found the study of the "total region" to be an elusive and frustrating undertaking. Probably the fact that few if any regions are entities within and unto themselves explains the greatest difficulty in comprehending fully their phenomena. That is, regions are subject to both extra and intra cybernations. Similarly, the transportation man dealing with kaleidoscopic spatial relationships found operating within a region has found that his attempts to understand and master the intricacies of his region, or sphere, of operations have usually escaped his efforts to incorporate them all in his decision-making processes. Today, however, high-speed communications, data processing, and selective computation equipment and techniques, when used in combination with the cybernetics concept, assist the geographer, economist, transportationist, and others who need to understand regions. Transportation researchers are coming to grips with many of the multifaceted problems inherent in regional operations as they must be carried out against the complex backdrop of their economic-geographic settings.

It is axiomatic that as long as mankind has wants and these wants can be filled only from unevenly located resources, there will be a continuing need for transportation. Historically, man's wants and use of resources to fill these wants have been regional in nature. Transportation systems and accompanying communication facilities are the arteries and nerves of the regional bodies sustaining man. Thus man's wants, resources, and regional settings are the parameters of any transportation system. Consequently, decision-making processes dealing with transportation systems must incorporate the ebb and flow of man's wants

---

1. A classic Commodity Flow study has been published: E. L. Ullman, *American Commodity Flow* (University of Washington Press, Seattle, Washington, 1957).

(the market place) with the resources (defined in its broadest sense) available through regional transportation systems to meet his wants.

Thus, the outer limits, or parameters, controlling transportation systems are regional in nature. As such, transportation's controls are more than operational and logistic in character. Such controls are also geographic, economic, military, political, and moral-psychological in nature. To date, most transportation-oriented work in cybernetics has dealt chiefly with rates, shipments, shipment schedules, market requirements, and economic forecasts. Omitted in the business-logistic decision-making processes have been environmental factors and interregional competition. To illustrate, the Carlsbad, New Mexico, area has been famous for its potash mines. The community and its people are now feeling the economic impact of closing mines because of lower-cost train-load rates which have been established from new Canadian potash deposits to major "Chemical Processing Regions," (combined with certain economies of scale and more modern loading facilities). Transportation costs have made the difference and the carrier(s) serving Carlsbad can either develop competitive services cost-wise or Carlsbad must find alternative employment opportunities (at least to the degree that the community's economic well-being depends on potash) or Carlsbad's economic position will decline. Cybernations emanate, in this case, from locations nearly 2000 miles distant; the implementation of a unit-train concept in one place has spelled economic ruin in a community thousands of miles away.

Within these outer limits, or controls, operate all of the transportation systems devised by man: the major, intermediate, and minor subsystems which are geographic, economic, military, political, moral-psychological, logistical, and/or operational in character. To date, most transportation-oriented work in cybernetics has been limited to equipment automation, paper processing and operational problems. Most data comes from production schedules, yards, car distributors and dispatchers. Before a complete system can be "cybernated" far more data will have to be processed, reduced to meaningful quantities or signals, and interjected into the operating and decision-making mechanism of a whole system—carrier or shipper. Again, most of these additional controls are regional in nature and, consequently, will have to come from the geographer, economist, military leader, political scientist, psychologist, as well as from the right-of-way and equipment engineer, traffic, and operational personnel.

Patterns of Regional Physical Controls and Feedback

Within a transportation system, anything that affects the movements of goods acts as a control on that system. Many controls are obvious and direct, others are extremely subtle and indirect. However, all inter-act with, or on, the system, and therefore need to be considered in developing a fully cybernated regional organism. Admittedly, the defini-tion of any system is arbitrary, but only within limits. In the case of a transportation artery and tributary arteries, the body served is the geographic region traversed or served by that transport system(s). Thus, and as pointed out, the basic or extreme controls in effect are physical and cultural.

geographic controls

Geographic controls affecting a transportation system are both physi-cal and cultural in nature. The physical geography controls are eight-fold: (1) climate and weather; (2) soils; (3) natural flora; (4) minerals; (5) water resources; (6) landforms; (7) natural fauna; and (8) loca-tion and spatial relationships. The cultural geography controls (discussed elsewhere throughout this text) are: (1) people; (2) houses and settle-ments; (3) features of production; and (4) features of transportation and telecommunications.

Climate and weather controls need to be read into a cybernated operation because of their impact on both commodity generation and operational requirements. Drouths, blizzards, cold fronts, storms, and prevailing winds all play major roles in what is grown, manufactured, or shipped in a region. Similarly, these elements affect operations in terms of out-of-pocket costs, disrupted schedules and rate levels. In extreme cases of natural catastrophes, routes may be damaged or destroyed by water, earthquake, or landslides.

Soil patterns or catenas, likewise, need to be measured, evaluated and programmed for productive capacities, fertilizer requirements, and for actual versus potential utilization. In this latter connection, political programs such as soil banks, crop quotas, or reforestation would, naturally, overlap. Land retirement, crop quota programs, even erosion rates are sufficiently rapid to consider soil a dynamic control affecting transportation systems. In regard to soils and other land use criteria, perhaps the most important input data would be derived from noting variations from a norm as registered on charts which show areas within regions according to their land use and yield records as compared with actual or anticipated production figures.

Similarly, data on forests and woodlot disease, cuttings, plantings, and board foot estimates could be used to develop regional input values for transportation systems. In recent years, quantitative techniques have been applied to geomorphological aspects of regions with interesting and valuable implications to man. For example, watershed soil removal, predictions of basin geometry, flooding, fertilizer requirements, and sequential development of terrain[2] all lead to the development of cyber-nations meaningful to business logistic decision processes. Even land fills (and predictions on garbage-refuse to fill them), island-forming tides, river improvements, beach changes, and shifting channels are but many kinds of dynamic geomorphic changes that affect logistical problems.[3] At the very minimum, physical geography shapes the technology of transportation and is therefore a cost factor.[4]

In review, physical geography factors are extremely powerful forces shaping the patterns of transportation. As environmental forces, they are permissive and cost factors, rather than prohibitive. And, as important as geographic factors might be in shaping transportation patterns, they are no more important than are business logistic controls.

Patterns of Business Logistic Controls and Feedback

Equally important with the geographic controls and limitations of a region are the operative business logistics controlling the transportation patterns of a region. Perhaps the array of business logistical controls is too lengthy to develop completely in this text. Still, a consideration of selected logistical controls provides worthwhile insights as to the causes or reasons behind existing transportation patterns and will serve to illustrate how such "business controls" act as cybernations often affecting an entire transportation system.

the marketing pattern of the firm

From the firm or shipper's point-of-view transportation increasingly bridges time and place discrepancies so that orderly production and marketing can take place. An overview of this requirement of business firms must include

    a. concentration/storing
    b. production
    c. storing/dissemination/timing of deliveries of goods or services
    d. market assorting
    e. market equalization

Business logistics encompasses all transportation/warehousing activities to include transport, materials handling, storage and related com-

2. George H. Dury, *Perspectives in Geomorphic Processes*, (Commission on College Geography, Resource Paper No. 3, Association of American Geographers, 1969), p. 27.

3. Meigs Field, Chicago; Kennedy Airport, New York: floods in the Mid-west, mud-slides in Southern California; plus Corps of Engineers harbor improvements and beach construction are additional points illustrating dynamic nature of geomorphic changes.

4. i.e.; Development of the S. S. *Manhattan* as a prototype to transport oil from the North Alaska Slope.

munications. As plant and warehouse locations affect these activities, their locations are integral to over-all business logistics planning.

In some firms, the production management point-of-view dominates and, in comparison, the market management of getting and filling orders may suffer (Figure 5.2). In other firms, the market management view dominates and production inputs suffer relatively (Figure 5.2). In the firm applying a total flow, or business logistics, concept the entire flow of goods is considered as one. The concept includes the inflow of raw materials, parts, and subassemblies as well as the outflow of the production or manufacturing effort. The total view includes materials handling, packaging and warehousing (See Figure 5.2).[5]

In this mental picture of a business logistics system many of the stages may not be owned by the firm. Their only control may be as a buyer of services; i.e., transportation, storage, packaging, etc. To assure a smooth flow and to control costs (in turn, to optimize profits) many firms integrate as many of these functions as possible. Toward this end, many firms own and operate their own warehouses, trucks, ships, barges, tank cars, gondolas, etc. At the same time, some firms find that it is more economical to rent, lease, or buy storage, materials handling and transportation from contract or common carriers or public warehousemen even though they sometimes lose control over location and give control of goods over to a third party for handling or transportation.

Demand for a certain goods or service is the strongest factor in determining a total business logistic pattern, and whether or not a firm is completely integrated or rents, leases, or buys storage and transportation: all aspects of the firm's total logistical pattern. If it is to be competitive (successful) it must consider the market place or demand.

analysis of demand for transport services

The demand of a routeway system's market area depends on its size, shape, and intensity. Size and shape are relatively easy to understand. All other things being equal, the larger the size, the greater the demand; in theory, a circle provides the optimum market area from a focal point. However, in practice Lösch, Isard, Hoover, and others theorize that a polygon, probably a hexagon, is the ideal market area to be served from a point.[6] In the case of a routeway, there would be a whole

---

5. The business logistics approach, although closely identifying with purchasing, production and selling, does not include these functions of the firm *per se.*
6. August Lösch, *The Economics of Location* (New Haven: University Press, 1952), pp. 414-421; Walter Isard, *Location and Space-Economy* (New York: John Wiley and Sons, Inc., 1956), pp. 266-281; and E. M. Hoover, *The Location of Economic Activity* (New York: McGraw-Hill Book Company, Inc., 1948), pp. 50-65 and pp. 219-224.

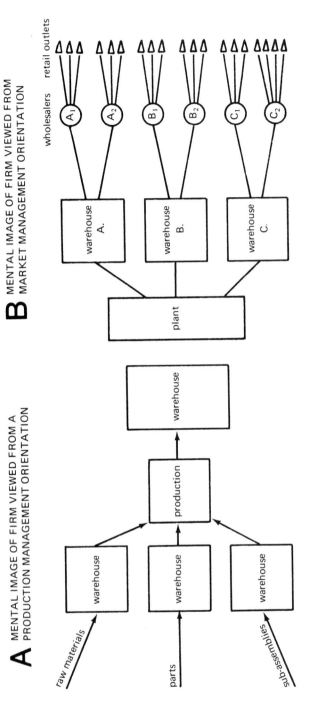

A MENTAL IMAGE OF FIRM VIEWED FROM A PRODUCTION MANAGEMENT ORIENTATION

Note: This pattern favors the even flow of goods and materials through production lines (all other factors being equal).

B MENTAL IMAGE OF FIRM VIEWED FROM MARKET MANAGEMENT ORIENTATION

Note: This pattern favors the even or timely movement of goods and materials to the customer (all other factors being equal).

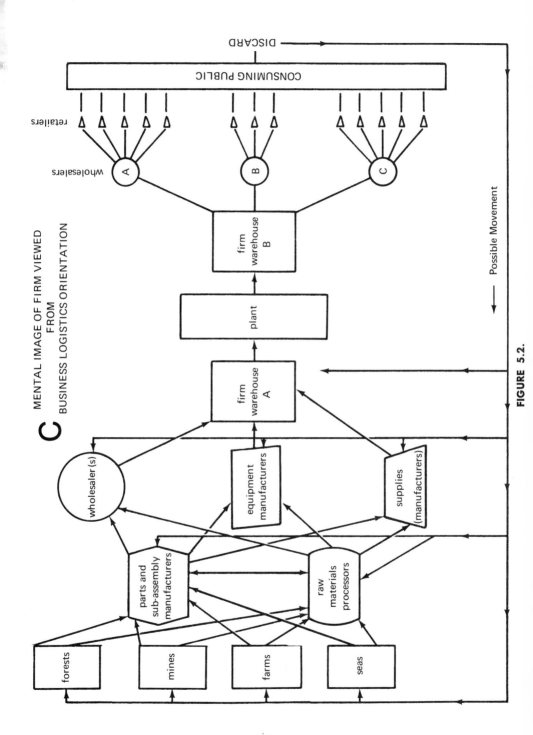

C MENTAL IMAGE OF FIRM VIEWED FROM BUSINESS LOGISTICS ORIENTATION

FIGURE 5.2.

71

series of overlapping market areas delimited by the dissemination patterns of a single good, commodity, or service. Thus, routeway market areas tend to be oblong in total outline, although in detail each of the oblong market areas has inner, agglomerated, more nearly circular submarket patterns. These mental pictures of market areas may be overgeneralized but they are useful in picturing the area serviced by a routeway. In any event, the intensity of the market is of far greater importance in analyzing demand.

The intensity of a carrier-market area is a product of three major interacting forces: (1) the spirit and educational levels of the people as measured by societal values (which, in turn, determine needs and wants); (2) the technology and skills of the people; and (3) the basic resource building blocks or geographic controls that are available to a people within a nation, subpolitical unit, or region (based on parameters other than political).[7]

The degree to which the three interacting forces differ from place to place sets the standard of comparative advantage for a given region and for each of its subregions as these might be restricted or shaped by transportation cost and time factors. In summary, it might be helpful to point out that, according to Greenhut, there are three categories of locational factors to be measured in determining the optimum site in a capitalistic economy.[8]

The demand factors include:
1. The shape of the demand curve.
2. The location of competitors.
3. The competitiveness of the industry in location and price.
4. The significance of proximity, type and speed of service.
5. The extent of the market area.
6. The relationship between personal contacts and sales.

The cost factors include:
1. The cost of land.
2. The cost of labor and management.
3. The cost of materials and equipment.
4. The cost of transportation.

The purely personal factors include:
The extent to which the minimax principle outweighs the quest for maximum profits. This principle includes:

---

7. As indicated on page 67, these are: (a) a favorable climate; (b) usable terrain; (c) soil type; (d) vegetation stages; (e) ores; (f) waterbodies; (g) native fauna; (h) location and spatial relationships.

8. Melvin Greenhut, *Microeconomics and the Space Economy.* (Scott Foresman and Company, Fair Lawn, N. J., 1963), Chapter 5.

1. The importance of psychic income (size of plant).
2. Environmental preferences.
3. The security motive.

How the transportation aspects of these locational factors affect plant location and, in turn, are affected by them forms a main theme of this text and are considered below.

transportation rates

Transportation rates in response to demands are the key factors producing routeways with their concentrated markets. As was pointed out in Chapter I, the basic transportation routeway pattern of the United States is based on the railroad pattern which existed at the turn of the century. Railroads did not then, nor do they now, charge the same rate on all shipments, either by the items moved or by the distance covered. Rather, the railroads have charged in accordance with (1) out-of-pocket costs; (2) value of service; (3) competition; and (4) what the traffic will bear. To accomplish this, railroads base their charges on (a) classification of the freight to be moved; (b) a series of rates for each class; and (c) established "commodity rates."[9] Thus, ratings and rates are two quite different things. The rate applies to a rating[10] and a distance. Rail classifications are different in each of the major geographic areas of the nation (Figure 5.3).

The rates that apply to the ratings set forth in a freight classification are published in Freight Tariffs and apply between specific points or districts. As important as ratings and rates have been in establishing today's transportation patterns, it is significant that in terms of volume, more than 95 per cent of all freight moves under commodity rates. For the most part commodity rates reflect a shipper's need to remain competitive at a given location and thus continue to generate traffic for a specific carrier serving that location.[11]

Rate territories have been established (Figure 5.3) because of variations in shipment patterns, both in terms of kinds of goods shipped, average distances goods are hauled, and attendant costs. Beginning with 1925, different classification and rate structures have evolved in South-

---

9. Rates quoted on a specific commodity, such as coal or grain.
10. There are many departures from published ratings known as "Exceptions to the Classifications." Where these are published, the exceptions take precedence over the classification.
11. Responsibility for establishment of a rate level usually (unless contested) resides in the carrier. The Interstate Commerce Commission does not usually set rates. Rather they approve or modify rates with the avowed goal of preventing practices destructive and harmful to the general good. Historically, the Interstate Commerce Commission has, as a matter of policy, attempted to maintain intra- and inter-modal competition.

ern, Eastern, New England, Southwestern, Central Freight Associations, and Western Transcontinental or Trunk Line Territories.

In all territories the rate structures have served to emphasize the routeway patterns. And, even though there are different structures prevailing in each of the aforementioned territories (plus a host of smaller territories and districts as well) there are a number of common characteristics.

FIGURE 5.3. Selected major Railroad freight classification territories.
Source: Information statement no. 4-64, issued by the Interstate Commerce Commission, May, 1964.

Among these is the development of a series of master distance scales for first class rates, applicable throughout the territory. Rates are customarily based upon a starting rate for terminal and clerical servicing, plus a charge for the first few (usually five) miles. Thereafter, additional charges are added for each five miles up to 100 miles, another series of rates are added for each 10 miles up to 240 miles, 20 mile increments (or fraction thereof) on all mileages up to 800 miles. Larger increments apply over 800. The impact, of course, is to favor traffic moving the greater distance along a routeway.

In addition, movement between centers of heavy traffic generation are customarily provided rate levels below that of traffic moving similar distances between points of lessor traffic densities. So-called key rates are established below the master mileage scale of rates and apply between ports and major terminal cities, river-crossing cities (gateways), etc. Such key rates are usually restricted to major routeways.

Giving further emphasis to the major routeways is the block (or step) application of these key rates. Such rates are applicable to all mainline points between a specified key point and the next key rate point to or from which lower key rates have been assigned. For example:

From Origin	To Points

	1.00			1.20
A	W	X	Y	Z

←————————————————————————→

Thus, all points from W to Z would be charged $1.00 per hundredweight. Thus, in effect, providing points such as X and Y with the same low rate enjoyed by W with the effect of stringing traffic-generating plants along the routeway A to Z. Also, in this regard, if a shipment is to be broken down into smaller units for reshipment, Z would be the desired location. A location at Z would allow shipments beyond and back into the W-Z area at a cost no greater than to reach W.

Differential rates,[12] too, in effect intensify concentration of economic activity along routeways. Rates to and from specified key points are sometimes constructed by subtracting differentials from the otherwise obtaining key rates. For the most part, these rate differentials are used to encourage the movement of traffic along major routes. The purpose, of course, is to increase traffic volumes so that, for example, a given freight train, its crew and power units will move longer trains and fuller cars. Thus train crews and other operational cost factors are maximized.

There are certain exceptions to these common characteristics of rates as listed. One class of exception is social factors. There are certain social forces that might result in the creation of rates that favor traffic away from routeways. As a matter of national, state, or local policy (sometimes the result of a court edict) making effective favorable rates to attain social goals in an accepted practice with certain understandable reservations on the part of the carriers. For example, rail carriers may be forced to maintain passenger service even though the result is financial loss. Other examples are the low rates on sulphur from such copper-producing areas as Ducktown, Tennessee. Without low rates on sulphur "processed out" during copper smelting processes the resultant sulphur could not be shipped economically to distant steel, rubber and chemical markets. Rather, the sulphur would have to be burned, leaving an acid fallout which, in the past, literally destroyed all vegetation for miles

---

12. A differential is a rate factor usually not available on local and feeder routes. These differentials are then subtracted from published key rates.

around the smelter. The fallout left the landscape so severely scarred and wasted that it appeared much like the surface of the moon.

schedules

Departure and arrival schedules and the scheduling of shipping quotas (see Appendix A) are two quite different aspects of transportation schedules which serve to reinforce routeway development.

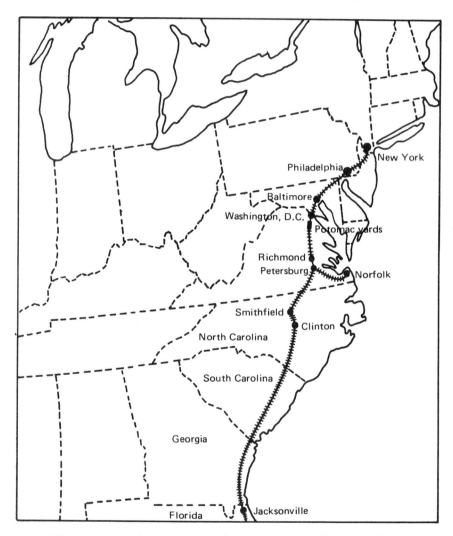

FIGURE 5.4. Map showing relationship of Potomac yards on mainline, east coast routeway and Norfolk, Virginia on a branchline to the east coast routeway. (Freight cars picked up in Florida, Georgia, South Carolina and North Carolina "block through" the Potomac yards to market cities.)

Departure and arrival schedules are often a determining factor in plant location and illustrate well the importance of routeway locations to industry. Because of the infinite variations and combinations of circumstance in which departure or arrival schedules favor routeway locations the principle is better detailed than generalized. For example, if a furniture manufacturer seeks an eastern location for a plant to serve the Philadelphia, Baltimore, New York markets, train schedules favor a location on the main line of the Eastern or Atlantic Coast routeway rather than a location in a city off of the routeway such as Norfolk, Virginia. Why?

In part the explanation rests on the marketing phenomena that furniture is often sold by using floor samples. Based upon the floor sample selected, orders are placed and the merchandise is then manufactured. Thus, if a firm is located in Norfolk, Virginia (off the mainline) as much as two days may be lost in transit if rail is used as compared with mainline locations even hundreds of miles further south. This delay results from the fact that late afternoon or evening trains leaving the Carolina locations are blocked through to Philadelphia or New York so that they arrive the next morning, whereas the Norfolk trains, departing on a branch line, connect with a mainline local at Petersburg, Virginia. The next morning these cars are moved to the Potomac Gravity Switchyards, located just south of Washington, D. C. In these yards, it usually takes a day to sort cars into trains for movement further north so that goods shipped via this route and schedule would not arrive in Philadelphia or New York until two days after the Carolina shipments would have been spotted in their market (destination) city for unloading. A two-day delay in delivery often loses a sale. (See Figure 5.4) Thus, this example illustrates the importance of routeway locations in terms of departure and arrival schedules.

In contrast, shipping schedules are also critical in determining a plant location or as a basis of comparing one location with other possible locations for a given plant site. Here again, the principle involved is better illustrated in detail rather than generalized and such an example is provided in Appendix A.

diversion and reconsignment

Diversion and reconsignment are two most important keys to an understanding of the role and function of routeways; for that matter, the ability of the United States industrialists to equalize prices throughout the nation. As a matter of custom, diversion and reconsignment are used interchangeably; in practice, there is a difference. The term "diversion" is the term used when a shipment has been directed from one geographic destination to another. Reconsignment refers to a change in the consignee of a shipment. Basically, under both diversion and reconsignment, shipments move at the regular published rates from origin to destination, plus very modest fees to cover any diversion or reconsignment costs. Thus, lettuce and other fresh produce can be shipped toward a market, still to be determined. Then, once loaded in refrigerator cars, the bill of lading can be used as collateral and the goods placed in motion. Depending on prevailing prices, these shipments can then be diverted to those cities (or markets) with the most favorable sales conditions. Usually those markets with the highest prices will soon have enough produce diverted or reconsigned to effect a lowering of prices so that produce may then be directed to other markets. The whole operation, in effect, is salutary in that it serves to equalize prices throughout the nation.

As the number of diversions or reconsignments are limited, the points at which they can be made are limited and are situated astride the major routeways. Thus, the existence of diversion or reconsignment points serves to make all other markets ancillary to these points, again a factor that intensifies routeway traffic and the market and other commercial activities integral to the routeway.

transit privileges

Transit rates apply to shipments stopped enroute to process, mix, combine, or package a product(s) before shipment is made to a final destination at a through rate which applies from an origin to destinations in its market area. The stopping in transit of pipe enroute from pipe mills and destined for use in pipelines or oil fields and the halting of grain enroute to market for cleaning, grading, grinding, mixing and other operations are two outstanding examples of in-transit activities. However, iron and steel fabrication, paint mixing and canning, food processing, textile printing and dyeing are other examples. In total, transit privileges have been granted to several hundred different kinds of commodities.

The obvious impact of transit rates is to cause raw or basic component shipments to move to a routeway. From these points, the altered goods move on toward market areas usually situated astride the same or connecting routeway. Furthering this effect of transit rates are certain rules usually followed when developing transit privileges.[13] The first of these is that backhaul or out-of-general direction hauls are discouraged and are granted only to meet competition or where the amount involved is relatively small in relation to the total movement.

---

13. Both carrier and the Interstate Commerce Commission view transit arrangements as a privilege granted by the carrier.

Even so, in such cases, there is usually a backhaul fee or penalty applied which tends to heighten the effect of floating goods toward a routeway and thence along that routeway.

Also, a second factor typical of transit operations which tends to reinforce the growth of routeways occurs when the inbound and outbound items do not carry the same rate. When this happens, the higher of the two rates is applicable, and, as this is almost without exception the processed article, this factor combined with the advantages of having goods under a bill of lading when enroute to market, tends to keep the floating-in shipments as short as possible and to lengthen the routeway portion of all transit related shipments.

regulation

Nearly all facets of government regulation tend to augment routeway patterns. Intended to protect, yet serve the general public, these regulations are set usually to assure safety, assure adequate and reasonable service, and to protect facilities. Safety regulations are intended only to protect life and property but in effect, in the process of enforcement especially in regard to trucks, tend to be administered through check points on the major routeways. Regulations to protect facilities, again especially in regard to highways, cause selected routeway development. For example, those states with the longest segments of interstate, for the most part built to higher specifications, allow the heaviest loads, permit higher speeds, and are more likely to allow the use of multiple trailers.

Economic regulation, intended to assure a high order of service at reasonable rates, also tends to develop routeway use. The requirement that a given level of service in terms of schedule frequency and dependability, stability of rates, avoidance of personal discrimination, and transport coordination are all easiest to implement along routeways rather than over broad areas. For example, certificates of public convenience and necessity are most often based on a route concept rather than to blanket an area and are granted accordingly.

Exemptions to regulation, too, work toward emphasizing routeways. Typical of such exemptions is the granting of authority to railroads, motor carriers, freight forwarders, and pick-up and delivery services to operate in an area terminal to a routeway. Even the agricultural exemptions provisions of the Interstate Commerce Act allowing farmers, cooperatives, and other haulers to move products of farm interest (but which in effect prohibit these same vehicles to move passengers or other goods for compensation) tend to cause commerce to gravitate toward routeways. This kind of exemption tends to float in products from broad areas of sparse or less intense economic activity to the routeway belts of greater economic activity.

total travel package

For many decades railroads have directly or indirectly been involved in providing a total travel package. To illustrate, hotels in or close to such scenic attractions as national parks were constructed by certain railroads to provide destinations for wanted passengers. Usually, these were constructed within relatively short distances of transcontinental routeways, thus serving to heighten routeway traffic. Similarly, Niagara Falls was billed as a national attraction and hotels and other facility construction was encouraged by a carrier serving a major routeway; still another example can be cited in that much of the Florida East Coast was developed by the Florida East Coast Railroad and eventually became an integral part of the Eastern Seaboard routeway.

Total, comparable activities are underway by major airlines. United Airlines is encouraging construction of ski lodges; Continental is building hotels and inns on distant Pacific islands in anticipation of being granted routes throughout much of the Pacific. In this instance, Vietnamese war-related contracts developed a capacity of equipment and personnel and the necessary experience to provide safe service over vast stretches of ocean air routes; thus, with any decrease in war activity, there will be an excess capacity to move passengers and material. Hence Continental is interested in developing new markets for its wartime-developed capabilities. The long-range impact of this kind of economic activity will serve to create the routeways of tomorrow very much as the railroads created the major domestic U S routeways of today.

Industrial development

As transportation tied production schedules to market demands it is not surprising to find that carriers are keenly interested in adding both dimensions to their routes of service. Consequently, in terms of industrial development efforts, transportation companies are, along with governmental agencies and utilities, among the leaders in their attempts to create the kind of total environment favorable to industry and commerce.

Carriers gamble hundreds of millions of dollars annually on Industrial Development. So keen has competition for new industries become that there is no longer any point in a carrier's management questioning, "Can our firm afford to invest in efforts to attract new traffic-generating industries?" to their areas of operations because, today, it is more logical to ask, "Can our firm afford *not* to enter the contest for new plants?"

This is, at least in part, behind the willingness of carriers to cooperate with community betterment programs within their spheres of interest. New tonnages are all too often related to the availability of certain cultural advantages—theatres, art galleries, libraries, museums and other cultural features—usually possible only in areas with growing dynamic economies. Similarly, basic to new tonnages for carrier growth are adequate schools, hospitals, roads, police, fire protection and good utility services.

Thus, carriers welcome new industries as an aid in diversifying and broadening tax bases to help community growth, even if they do not always contribute directly to the volume of freight to be moved. For carriers are aware of and appreciate the fact that progressive communities do eventually, even if indirectly, add to their freight and travel markets.

Summary

Business logistics, through its many cybernations, tends to touch every aspect of the economy. Business logistics/transportation tend to both shape the patterns of goods and passengers in motion and, at the same time, be shaped by them. The most obvious evidence of the pattern produced are the routeways: routeways which seemingly feed on and are augmented and reinforced by the very forces which brought them into being in the first place. The sum impact of routeways is found in the fact that they, in turn, form the framework of towns, cities, and metropolitan conglomerations (the strip cities). The routeways are very much part and parcel of the nation's metropolitan enigma and, as such, are increasingly receiving national attention in the hope of alleviating many of the nation's urban, security, and pollution problems. Toward this end, national policies must be found if transport contributions are to be maximized for the good of the entire nation.

Chapter 6

Summary/Conclusion—
An Evolving National Transportation
and Business Logistics Pattern

The national transportation and business logistic pattern as it is today, although built upon and evolving from the one carrier era of the beginning of the century, bears little relationship to that era. Furthermore, it fails to parallel even the pattern which obtained during the 1930's when highway transport came of age. The geographical dispersion of the shipping public has followed the routeways so that today's markets (and metropolitan/urban centers) are aligned along and, in large measure, are conterminous with the major routeways (see Figure 6.1). Since the turn of the century, transportation, although keeping apace of production and marketing in terms of technology has not been allowed to advance equally as far operationally. This has been due, at least in part, to regulation design; regulation to protect competing goods, ostensibly for the public good. The long range impact of such regulation has been a major factor holding back changes in transport operations.

Problems compounded by the sheer number of people and mass of vehicles and freight to be moved, on the one hand, and an inability to operationally optimize or even use modern technology, on the other hand, add to man's frustrations. The fact that rates, ratings and routings, as historically evolved, do not lend themselves to computer techniques; that even though men can move quickly between cities he is choked to a standstill within cities; that the technical ability to move peoples and goods from place to place rapidly produces unacceptable levels of pollution or confusion, are causing widespread concern about transportation. Within the last decade this concern, in turn, has resulted in:

1. a Federal Department of Transportation headed by a presidential cabinet member;
2. a broad recognition and acceptance of the science/art known as "business logistics" or "physical distribution";

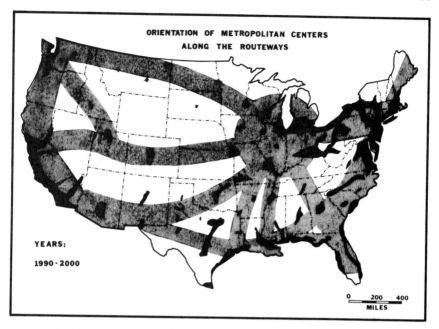

FIGURE 6.1. Orientation of metropolitan centers along the major route-ways.

3. numerous carrier mergers;
4. emphasis on specialized, long-distance, commodity and/or container movements; and
5. various kinds of coordinated transport services.

These, in turn, are leading to a transport revolution which will produce transportation companies operating multivalent distribution centers under needed new national and state transport policies. Such policies will encourage a wider use of containerization and simplified pricing, and will give competition a freer hand. Thus, new patterns will evolve not only in spite of, but also because of, powerful conflicts in transport policies now in progress.

A Federal Department of Transportation

The investment of federal, state and local governments, on the one hand, with those of privately operated carriers (even though under some degree of regulation), on the other, has reached such a level that the federal government has been compelled to combine the national effort under one cabinet officer so that the left hand might know what the right is doing. After all, the privilege of benefiting from rights-of-way, airports, highways, port terminals, waterways, and such supporting services as a Bureau of Public Roads, Civil Aeronautics Administration, and many other services provided under the governmental aegis belongs to all citizens, not just the carriers and/or shippers. At the same time, collectively, various governmental agencies constitute the nation's largest shipper. Thus a Federal Department of Transportation has been authorized by Congress. Indeed, an act was signed into law in October, 1966; its first Secretary of Transportation, Alan S. Boyd, was appointed by President Johnson in November, 1966. Under a unifying cabinet officer there should be a reduction in the forces which have kept the industry divided by carrier mode.

Business Logistics or Physical Distribution

The advent of the computer and electronic data processing have made possible the *business logistics* (or *physical distribution*) *concept*. Business logistics is a mixture of science and art dealing with the total flow of goods to include the accumulation of materials for processing and the distribution of manufactured items. Formerly, the combined facets of these shipments were too numerous to record and process as a series of cybernated movements. Consequently, they were handled separately, shipment by shipment. Today, however, pertinent data and shipping papers can be prepared by machine (computer) techniques. As the total patterns of shipments are recognized and eventually better understood, all aspects of movement will be affected including:

1. Plant Location
2. Warehouse Location
3. Distribution Center Location
4. Carrier selection
5. Route selection
6. Scheduling
7. Cost analyses of:
    a. rates
    b. tariffs
    c. billing
    d. loading
    e. shipping instructions
    f. packaging
    g. leasing or buying equipment
    h. materials handling

The total impact of these developments will be to increase capacities and volumes, further intensifying traffic along existing routeways.

Carrier Mergers

As operational techniques emerge in regard to the use of larger equipment, larger and faster terminals (including switching operations), coordinated equipment, and longer hauls, carriers operating along the same routeways have found that many economies can be enjoyed through mergers. Central-traffic-control means one track can be used instead of four; the diesel engine with its favorable characteristics of reliability and greater range between needed service points means that power units must be provided greater distances and more tonnage to optimize their use. Similarly, the use of multiple-truck trailer units, coordinated transportation (i.e., Trailer-on-Flatcar) all mean that significant savings in labor-loading facilities and maintenance, plus an increased use of equipment, can result through mergers. Again, the routeway pattern is intensified by reducing their geographic coverage or width, a logical result of reduced rail mileage or concentration of truck traffic on a relatively few interstate highways.

Emphasis on Specialized, Long-distance, Commodity and/or Container Movements

At the present, few carriers find it profitable to haul small and/or shorthaul shipments. In most carrier situations, volume and long-distance movements are the most profitable. Thus, even though it may not be intentional or overt, carriers often fail to service small shipments and/or communities. More and more small shipments are, in effect, falling to such firms as the (Railway) Express Agency,[1] Greyhound Bus Lines, or Freight Forwarders. The latter serves to consolidate shipments into volume shipments and then, at a destination terminal, break bulk.

Collectively, these economic forces tend to intensify routeway development. This intensification results from the fact that less than carload (LCL) orders, truckload (LTL) and packages first move to collecting terminals on a routeway. There they are placed in containers, cars, or truck vans for destination terminals (again usually on a routeway) to be broken down into smaller units for eventual delivery. Coordinated transport service has a similar impact on transportation patterns.

coordinated transport service

The term coordinated transport service is used even though it means many different things to different people. The term has been defined as the "physical integration of particular facilities of two or

---

1. The Railway is now a misnomer as this firm uses highway and air as well as rail.

more carriers without the integration of the carrier management and policies."[2] The objective of coordination is to provide better optimums of shipping patterns for the shipping public in terms of costs whether these costs are related to rates, routes, schedules, equipment or mode. For various reasons certain carriers have resisted providing coordinated transport. For example, railroads have been forbidden by Congress to reduce the number of employees.[3] Thus, if railroads must maintain a set payroll level, why should they feel any need to provide a cooperative service which might well cause them to lose income?

However, today, there are forces acting on carriers which will, in a relatively brief time, effect a much higher degree of coordination than has been true in the past. The most important of these forces is the growth in use of equipment that provides intermodal compatibility. The idea, of course, is not new, but the technique and equipment adequate to effect those techniques are fairly recent in origin. Today, trailer-on-flatcar is widely available and used,[4] rail cars, trucks, and containers are moved by water and containers are moved by air. Each of these movements must be coordinated between at least two carrier modes under the definition provided above. In any event, coordination to be effective must operate where volumes of traffic warrant the investment and use of automated equipment and containers (with container pooling), thus serving to strengthen already existing routeway patterns.

Today, intermodal compatibility is an accomplished fact for many facets of transportation. A key to its success today, and in the future, is the availability of highly automated terminals with requisite warehouses and storage yards equipped to receive, package, sort, store, label, schedule, and dispatch to any one of the several carriers serving a given terminal.

the distribution center

Today, and to a much higher degree tomorrow, the intermodal distribution center is a computerized interchange facility to effect transfers of freight between carriers to include transfers from one mode to another. To envisage what will be required to compete in the future

---

2. Robert D. Brooks, *Coordinated Transportation Service—a Railroad Point-of-View*. Proceedings of the Sixteenth Annual Transportation Conference and Solzberg Memorial Lecture, Syracuse University, November 9, 1964, (The Business Research Center, Syracuse University), p. 14.

3. U. S. Government Printing Office, *The Emergency Transportation Act of 1933*, Section 7 (b) (Washington, D. C., 1934).

4. Here again the concept is not new, having been used during the War Between the States (1860's), by the Long Island Railroad at the turn of the present century, and the Chicago, North Shore Lines 1925-1928. But, today, the same five to seven different categories of TOFC services are available almost nationwide.

one must picture a computerized system using unitized loads where movement is activated through computer commands and processed decisions (see Figure 6.2).

In terms of operating an intermodal terminal, it is only logical to assume that they will be managed by so-called "transportation companies" which would also manage (probably even own) the carriers which serve the terminal. Thus, such a firm could offer a shipper a complete logistical or physical distribution package. The package would include the gathering, stopping, storage, sorting, grading, packaging, labeling, scheduling, loading and dispatching of goods for shipment. To be successful, the location of such terminals becomes a vital consideration, and, in this regard, an appreciation of the routeway's role in the total economic scheme becomes essential.

locations

Major distribution center locations will be, of course, a key to their future success. Routeway intersects or convergence points suggest logical points in terms of carrier services and markets to be served (see Figure 6.2). Although the major metropolitan centers constitute much of the market, distribution centers would in practice serve regional markets. Thus feeder carriers, especially highway and air, must consider these locations as regional focal points. Here, again, as Figure 6.2 shows, the major routeway intersects also serve as logical regional focal points.

needed new national and state transportation policies

Obviously, when such a major industry as transportation arrives at a point in time when historic alignments, orientations, and working patterns are being overturned, powerful vestiges are sometimes overrun in the process. That the affluent and those with vested interests will resist impending changes which they might see as a threat to their current economic position is axiomatic. Usually when impending changes produce conflicts in status the conflicts are first recognized as a specific issue. These are then translated into philosophies which are used in the political arena where they are translated into new or changed governmental policies. In turn, new or modified statutes and laws, rules and regulations are promulgated to implement the new or revised policies. Thus, today, as a result of technological advances which enable quick responses to cybernations, improved communications, rapid data processing, improved equipment (size and loading/unloading devices), and numerical or computer controls, the old rate structure and operational alignments are beginning to crumble. Shippers (including government as the nation's largest shipper) are clamoring for new policies, making it possible to optimize the application of known technologies to total

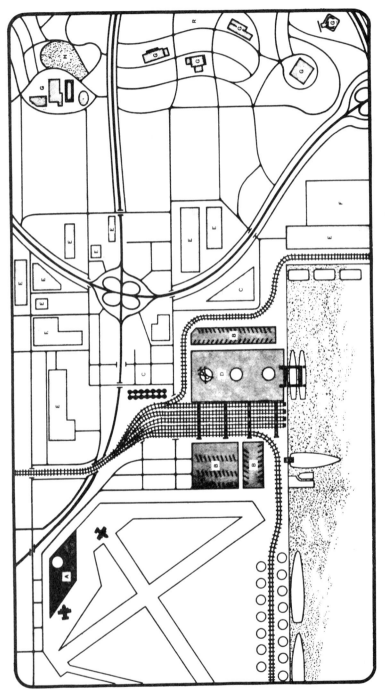

FIGURE 6.2. Schematic drawing of an intermodal terminal.

Source: O. H. Overmyer, "The Intermodal Terminal Complex, New Hub of the Wheel of Commerce," *Handling and Shipping,* December, 1968. p, 34-5.

transportation operations. Also, in their search for economies, legislative bodies are seeking ways to reduce or prevent duplications of transportation investments whatever the form, whether rail, highway, airfield, or waterway facilities. Currently, legislative bodies evidence special interest in those measures aimed at policy dealing with mass transit problems in urban areas. With such an environment, nationally, it is not surprising to find many conflicts in transport policies. And, with those conflicts in mind, appreciations and understandings of routeways as they exist today are germane to most considerations as to just what national policies *are* to be adopted. Some of the conflicts currently under debate merit discussion.

Private Enterprise vs. Government Ownership

Should national policies further the cause and protect private enterprise competition even though the routeways in terms of rights-of-way, certificates of convenience and necessity, airway operations, waterway maintenance, and highway investment and control are very much functions of government? Obviously, competition is keenest under private entrepreneurship, but many will argue, "Can we continue to afford this luxury? Can we continue to be the only nation in the world with private management of the transport function?" It can also be most effectively asked, "Can we afford not to abet and encourage private ownership and management of transportation in this country and still maintain our cherished freedoms of rights to move freely and rights to communicate freely?" In the final analysis it will probably be decided that private enterprise and competition provide the only real market measures for the distribution or allocation of resources whether these be a service such as transportation or raw or manufactured goods.

Should Carriers be Allowed to Own, Manage and Operate More than One Mode so as to Actually Operate as a "Transportation Company" rather than as a Single-Mode Carrier?

As has been pointed out, railroads already operate trucks as well as rail equipment. Airways are almost helpless to fly freight without trucks. Similarly, barges, by and large, require connecting truck, rail, pipeline, or conveyor systems to be effective. And, by their nature, routeways consist of different kinds of carriers. These factors, when combined with the widespread use of containers (or vans) moving on trailer, large deep-sea vessel or air, or in combinations of these modes, suggest that the era of the transportation company is, in effect, actually here and needs only governmental recognition. Still, there are affluent and interested parties that argue that, chiefly due to their size financially, this means that railroads will "swallow" all other modes.

Therefore, national transportation policies should protect their particular operations. Still others argue that distribution centers or freight forwarders can perform the needed coordination function and that this would still maintain the favorable feature of intermodal competition as an effective means of controlling shipping costs. These same individuals would argue that a monopoly is likely to develop under a transportation company policy and that the nation's experience under a one-carrier system was stifling to the economy.[5]

Should Governmental Agencies Support One Carrier in Contrast to Taxing (Unfairly) Other Modes?

Here again, the routeways receive most of the funds invested in interstate highways, airways, and waterways. And, conversely, the railroads pay the heaviest taxes to operate in these areas. Thus, the routeway concept is basic to any consideration of the relative merits of governmental transportation investments and taxing policies.

The Question of Transportation Management's Obligations to Society

Should the managers of the nation's transportation carriers be free to operate in such a way as to capitalize on the large volume, long-haul of the heavily trafficked routeways, or should they be forced to provide comparable service to points remote from volume-generating routeways?

How to Price Transportation Services

This question is a basic conflict between the two extremes of charging what the traffic will bear, on the one hand, with a flat weight/volume/distance rate, on the other. Obviously, the settings of rates along routeways must consider quite a different set of conditions in terms of volume, weight, schedules, equipment needs, and requisite terminal facilities than exists in off-routeway situations. The fact that plants, jobs, and even entire communities are predicated on existing rate structures, causes rate changes to have serious and farreaching effects. Thus, perhaps a secondary-level question of whether to simplify rates so that they may be more easily and quickly adapted to computer and data-processing applications, is in conflict with the very existence of communities and all of the hardships that their possible demise might entail.

Should Intermodal Coordination Be Forced?

This is a current question in conflict that has already been discussed.[6]

---

5. See Chapter III, especially reference to transportation produced depression of 1906-1908, p.
6. See this chapter, p. 89.

Should Intramodal Competition Be Maintained?

At present it is, by national policy, being maintained; but, at the same time, it is, as a policy, under erosion. Mergers are taking place but currently are being controlled so that intramodal competition is being maintained along the major routeways. However, away from the major routeways, particularly in isolated, small communities, the available traffic is often thrown to one company. This method gives a specific company all, or most, of the freight volume from a given town. Even where there may be more than one truck line serving a community, the terminal is usually managed (controlled) by one truck line. In these matters, routeway locations present quite a different mix of factors to be considered than off-routeway locations, so that clearcut resoltuions of this type of conflict are most difficult of attainment.

What of the Conflicts Concerning "Personal" Rate Discrimination?

All rates by their very nature are discriminatory. Admittedly, most rates usually discriminate in terms of volume, density, weight, insurability, direction, etc. Thus, routeway areas receive favorable discriminations as compared with off-routeway locations. Significantly, since the Transportation Act of 1920 and its subsequent revisions, personal discrimination has been fairly well controlled; but, today, the emerging conglomerates or stock holding/management firms are again raising questions of a personal discrimination nature. Can a firm which holds controlling interests in a carrier and, at the same time, controls firms that are shippers of freight, serve the general public fairly and guarantee that the carrier(s) which they control will not be operated to stifle competition? It is conceivable that the power of such vested interest might operate even in opposition to the very forces which have created routeways. Solutions to these conflicts of conglomerates are not evident, nor are they likely to be easily resolved.

It is not intended that this list of existing conflicts in transportation policies be complete. Rather, it is intended that they indicate the seriousness and breadth of such conflicts. There are many more. The question of government agencies collecting users charges from carriers using waterways, airports, ports, or roads is mostly timely. The question of whether or not railroads have the right to reduce labor levels and costs below certain historical minimums and how shipments should be allocated by carriers to best serve the national interest are typical of the many, many conflicts within the transport industry. Clearly, the routeway concept relates to many of them. Workforce reductions by railroads in urban centers as contrasted with workforce reductions in outlying villages or towns are very different matters in their impacts on local economies. Similarly, the collection of user charges from a heavily trafficked routeway is quite a different matter from what might be possible where traffic demands do not warrant the imposition of such charges. Thus if conflicts in transportation policy eventually are to be settled wisely, considerations and appreciation of the nature of routeways and the role of routeways in the national scheme of things takes on significant proportions.

conclusions

This study has intended to show that the ebb and flow of people and goods, transportation patterns, when considered as an adjunct to other functions (political, economic, social or military) shape greatly the pattern of nearly all of man's activities. By reducing the ceaseless, seething, kaleidoscopic ebb and flow of people and goods to the routeway pattern the study attempts to reduce a vast field to something more nearly comprehensible. In turn, to understand the pattern, it is necessary to see that the pattern's basic outline is based upon an era in this nation's history when rails were dominant. Thus the rail routeways of the early years of this century still constitute the major trunks of today's pattern even though these patterns have been modified by water, highway, pipeline and air developments. Relating to the routeway system, a cybernetic business logistics (or physical distribution) system has evolved. Increased efficiencies, based on improvements in data processing, computer-controls, faster communications, improved operational techniques, larger equipment, more power, and more reliable power, have combined to make possible a faster and more efficient national marketing pattern. In turn, this development now calls for improved distribution centers through which to better coordinate carriers and effect a more optimum marketing system which optimizes the the means for industries to:

1. collect materials needed in production or service;
2. disseminate goods and services;
3. provide a more complete assorting system; and
4. equalize opportunities to acquire goods and services.

Transportation is the key to accomplishing these marketing goals, and as transportation differs from place to place and, at the same time, serves to equalize differences from place to place its geographic qualities must be understood if major national (and international) conflicts in transport policies are to be resolved in those ways which will best serve man in the attainment of his wants, needs and goals. Toward this end, the routeway concept has been presented in this study.

Appendix A

Assume that a firm is presently operating two factories, one in Houston and another in South Norfolk. Its products are marketed through four warehouses: Chicago, Pittsburgh, Cincinnati and Toledo. The demands of these four market areas promise to exceed present plant capacities within four years. At present, one site at Memphis and another at St. Louis are receiving serious consideration as a possible location for the third plant. Your problem: ascertain which of the two sites is the lowest-cost in terms of transportation expenses from existing and planned plants to warehouses in the four market areas. (For purposes of this illustration, costs other than for transportation are not a consideration.)

Calculations assume a 40-hour work week and 52 week work year. The answer should be given in terms of transportation savings which can be obtained in the first full year the new plant will be in operation.

Chart I provides the basic data for the problem. It locates the existing and proposed plants, also the warehouses. In addition, it indicates hourly plant output and warehouse requirements, in units, and lists the per unit freight costs.

It should be emphasized that the problem has been selected for its simplicity. Actually, it can be solved by inspection, thus making it easier to see how the method works.

CHART I

Basic Data

To/From	Houston	South Norfolk	St. Louis	Memphis	Warehouse Quotas as Units
Warehouses In					
Chicago	110	160	(80)	(90)	350
Cincinnati	105	100	(85)	(70)	300
Toledo	140	150	(100)	(105)	200
Pittsburgh	125	90	(110)	(115)	150
Plant Capacities In Units	200	350	(450)	(450)	1000

Freight rates shown in cents per unit

Developing the Answer

From the point-of-view of transportation costs, St. Louis is the better of the two sites. A decision in favor of St. Louis will result in a savings of $20 per operating hour or $41,600 annually, or nearly $500,000 in the first ten years of operating the new plant.

The above solution was derived mathematically with pencil and paper. To start the problem an initial shipping schedule meeting all existing production and warehouses quotas as well as the planned quotas for the proposed plants and warehouses must be set. The first schedule is established by inspection, regardless of cost. To begin with, it is usually best to either build from existing movements or assume that each plant will supply as much of its output as possible to the closest warehouse, then apportion its remaining output to the next nearest warehouse so as to fulfill all warehouse requirements. The only precaution is to fill each warehouse to capacity before going on to the next warehouse. Chart II shows a trial shipping schedule.

CHART II

Trial Shipping Schedule

To/From	Houston	South Norfolk	St. Louis	Memphis	Total
Warehouses In					
Chicago	200	150			350
Cincinnati		200	(100)	(100)	300
Toledo			(200)	(200)	200
Pittsburgh			(150)	(150)	150
Total	200	350	(450)	(450)	1000

Proposed Movements Indicated in Units

In this example, present plant capacities are assigned to meet anticipated warehouse requirements depending on the method to indicate
optimum schedules for each of the proposed plants.

Our next step is to construct a chart showing what are termed row
and column values. As shown in Chart III, only those rates applying
to movements scheduled in Chart II are used to determine these values.
These rates are read from the corresponding locations on Chart I.

CHART III

Applicable Rates for Movements Shown in Chart II
A. St. Louis Schedule

To/From	Houston	South Norfolk	St. Louis	Row Value
Warehouses In				
Chicago	110	160		60
Cincinnati		100	85	0
Toledo			100	15
Pittsburgh			110	25
Column Value	50	100	85	

B. Memphis Schedule

To/From Warehouses In	Houston	South Norfolk	Memphis	Row Value
Chicago	110	160		60
Cincinnati		100	70	0
Toledo			105	35
Pittsburgh			115	45
Column Value	50	100	70	

Row values are arbitrarily assigned. (In connection with this problem it is necessary to establish separate row values for St. Louis and Memphis, keeping in mind that only one of these proposed plants is to become operative.) Next assign column values so that the sums of the row and column values will equal the values of each respective square of the chart.

Row and column data can be derived in any order and both positive and negative numbers can be used. Any inability to complete this data indicates that either an error has been made or that degeneracy is present.[1]

After correcting errors or adjusting for degeneracy, the next step is to construct a cost chart (Chart IV). This is done by filling in all blank squares with the sums of appropriate row and column figures.

1. If no error has been made then degeneracy is present and the following measures should be taken: If the number of plants is smaller than the number of warehouses, divide one unit of shipment by twice the number of plants. (If shipments are measured to the tenth of a ton, for example, divide 1/10 ton (not 1 ton) by twice the number of plants.) Take any convenient number smaller than this quotient and add it to the capacity of each plant; add the same total amount to the capacity of any one warehouse. If the number of warehouses is less than the number of plants, then reverse the rule. Proceed with the solution.

CHART IV

Actual and Projected Transporation Costs

A. St. Louis Schedule

To/From	Houston	South Norfolk	St. Louis	Row Value
Warehouses In				
Chicago	110	160	(145)	60
Cincinnati	50	100	85	0
Toledo	65	115	100	15
Pittsburgh	75	125	110	25
Column Value	50	100	85	

B. Memphis Schedule

To/From	Houston	South Norfolk	Memphis	Row Value
Warehouses In				
Chicago	110	160	130	60
Cincinnati	50	100	70	0
Toledo	85	135	105	35
Pittsburgh	95	(145)	115	45
Column Value	50	100	70	

By comparing Chart IV with Chart I we can refine the shipping schedule so as to evolve the least-cost operation. Keep in mind that St. Louis and Memphis data are to be treated separately, each to be considered in light of already existing plant capacities. A comparison of Charts IV and I indicates the optimum point(s) at which to begin our refinement process. This point is revealed by that square of Chart IV having the greatest excess over the corresponding rate in Chart I. In this connection one method is to encircle or place parentheses or curved marks around that square. Value differences as shown on Chart IV, in excess of those shown on Chart I, represents money to be saved. In this example the St. Louis-Chicago square in Chart IV is to be placed in parentheses marks; and, in the Memphis series shown on Chart IV B, square South Norfolk-Pittsburgh exceeds by the greatest amount corresponding number on Chart I, an indication that the next trial schedule adjustment should begin in this square.

To determine what subsequent changes must be made in the two plant combinations, so as to determine an optimum schedule of each for comparison, construct Charts V A and V B. These are based on Chart II.

CHART V

Work Chart for First Revised Shipping Schedule

A. St. Louis Schedule

To/From	Houston	South Norfolk	St. Louis	Total
Warehouses In				
Chicago	(200)	150-x	+x	350
Cincinnati		200+x	100-x	300
Toledo			(200)	200
Pittsburgh			(150)	150
Total	200	350	450	1000

B. Memphis Schedule

To/From	Houston	South Norfolk	Memphis	Total
Warehouses In				
Chicago	(200)	(150)		350
Cincinnati		200-x	100+x	300
Toledo			(200)	200
Pittsburgh		+x	150-x	150
Total	200	350	450	1000

After constructing Chart V a plus x is placed in the square in which the row and column value of Chart IV exceeds the corresponding value on Chart I by the greatest number. In other words, the plus x should be placed in the squares encircled on Chart IV. In this case the difference in Chart IV A is 65 cents and means that 65 cents will be saved for every unit diverted to this new route. The question then. Is how much can be redirected to take advantage of this savings and still remain within the specified plant capacities and warehouse requirements? X

represents the sum that can profitably be diverted and after placing the plus x in the appropriate square, the value of x is determined as follows:

1. Encircle all numbers in Chart V A standing alone in their row or column;
2. Now, treat each encircled number as though they were non-existent, and again encircle all numbers standing alone in their row or column;
3. Repeat until all possible numbers have been encircled;
4. As the chart now shows x number of units are to be diverted from present consignments to the Chicago warehouse, the fact that the number in the St. Louis-Cincinnati is not encircled indicates that here is the logical source of x, so place a minus x after the 100 in that square;
5. Adding x to the Chicago warehouse overloads it by that amount, therefore, the same amount must be diverted from another plant. In this case, the encircled 150 in the South Norfolk-Chicago square indicates that here are the x number of units to be diverted. Thus, place a minus x after the 150 in that square.
6. As a result of diverting x units from South Norfolk to Chicago, the South Norfolk plant now has an x number of units in excess; and, as x units have been diverted from the Cincinnati warehouse, these can be replaced by shipments from South Norfolk.
7. The value of x is determined by examining all the squares in which we have written a minus x, the smallest number in such a square is the value of x. In this example, the value of x is 100.
8. Now substituting 100 as the value of x, construct CHART VI.

CHART VI

First Revised Shipping Schedule

A. St. Louis Schedule

To/From	Houston	South Norfolk	St. Louis	Row Value
Warehouses In				
Chicago	200	50	100	350
Cincinnati		300		300
Toledo			200	200
Pittsburgh			150	150
Total	200	350	450	1000

B. Memphis Schedule

To/From	Houston	South Norfolk	Memphis	Total
Warehouses In				
Chicago	200	150		350
Cincinnati		50	250	300
Toledo			200	200
Pittsburgh		150		150
Total	200	350	450	1000

To determine further adjustments this process is repeated until all rates indicated are less than those shown in CHART I. To do this, construct CHART VII by copying the applicable rates from CHART I for the revised schedule as shown in CHART VI. Underline the rates applying to movements shown on CHART VI. Then fill in the rest of the data as was done in CHART IV.

CHART VII

Actual and Projected Routes

A. St. Louis Schedule

To/From	Houston	South Norfolk	St. Louis	Row Value
Warehouses In				
Chicago	110	160	80	60
Cincinnati	50	100	20	0
Toledo	130	180	100	80
Pittsburgh	140	(190)	110	90
Column Value	50	100	20	

B. Memphis Schedule

To/From	Houston	South Norfolk	Memphis	Row Value
Warehouses In				
Chicago	<u>110</u>	<u>160</u>	(130)	90
Cincinnati	50	<u>100</u>	<u>70</u>	30
Toledo	85	<u>135</u>	<u>105</u>	65
Pittsburgh	40	<u>90</u>	60	20
Column Value	20	70	40	

Another revision on each schedule is indicated; we construct CHART VIII.

CHART VIII

Workchart for Second Revision of Shipping Schedule

A. St. Louis Schedule

To/From	Houston	South Norfolk	St. Louis	Total
Warehouses In				
Chicago	(200)	$50-x$	$100+x$	350
Cincinnati		(300)		300
Toledo			(200)	200
Pittsburgh		$+x$	$150-x$	150
Total	200	350	450	1000

B. Memphis Schedule

To/From	Houston	South Norfolk	Memphis	Total
Warehouses In				
Chicago	(200)	$150-x$	$+x$	350
Cincinnati		$50+x$	$250-x$	300
Toledo			(200)	200
Pittsburgh		(150)		150
Total	200	350	450	1000

Similarly we solve for the correct decision and for the value of x as was done with CHART V. The value of x is now 50 and a new routing schedule, CHART IX, is constructed.

CHART IX

Second Revised Shipping Schedule

A. St. Louis Schedule

To/From	Houston	South Norfolk	St. Louis	Total
Warehouses In				
Chicago	200		150	350
Cincinnati		300		300
Toledo			200	200
Pittsburgh		50	100	150
Total	200	350	450	1000

B. Memphis Schedule

To/From	Houston	South Norfolk	Memphis	Total
Warehouses In				
Chicago	200		150	350
Cincinnati		200	100	300
Toledo			200	200
Pittsburgh		150		150
Total	200	350	450	1000

Again reproduce the applicable rates for movements indicated in CHART IX and compute appropriate values as shown in CHART X. Next compute the rate values for the rest of the squares—underlining those that apply to the movement of goods shown in CHART IX. Next, compare X A with I and X B with I. The greatest differences between X A and I is in the Houston-Cincinnati square indicating a need for a third revised schedule for the St. Louis pattern. However, all rates in X B are equal to or lower than corresponding rates in CHART I, hence the underlined rates, when applied to the movements shown on IX B, form the lowest cost shipping schedule for the Memphis combination.

CHART X

Rates on Chart IX Movements

A. St. Louis Schedule

To/From	Houston	South Norfolk	St. Louis	Row Value
Warehouses In				
Chicago	110	60	80	20
Cincinnati	(150)	100	120	60
Toledo	130	80	100	40
Pittsburgh	140	90	110	60
Column Value	90	40	60	

B. Memphis Schedule

To/From	Houston	South Norfolk	Memphis	Row Value
Warehouses In				
Chicago	110	120	90	40
Cincinnati	90	100	70	20
Toledo	125	135	105	55
Pittsburgh	80	90	60	10
Column Value	70	80	50	

CHART XI shows the first step toward making a third revised schedule for the St. Louis combination.

CHART XI

Third Revised Shipping Schedule for
The St. Louis Combination

To/From	Houston	South Norfolk	St. Louis	Total
Warehouses In				
Chicago	200-x		150+x	350
Cincinnati	+x	300-x		300
Toledo			(200)	200
Pittsburgh		50+x	100-x	150
Total	200	350	450	1000

Adjusting for x as done in previous revisions we find that x-100 and the adjusted schedule is shown in CHART XII.

CHART XII

Third Revised Shipping Schedule for
The St. Louis Combination

To/From	Houston	South Norfolk	St. Louis	Total
Warehouses In				
Chicago	100		250	350
Cincinnati	100	200		300
Toledo			200	200
Pittsburgh		150		150
Total	200	350	450	1000

For a third time, we extract those rates from CHART I which apply to the movements under consideration—these are shown in CHART XIII. Again, appropriate row values are computed, see CHART XIII; and the empty squares completed with the newly computed row and column values.

CHART XIII

Rates Applying to the Third Revised Shipping Schedule for
The St. Louis Combination

To/From	Houston	South Norfolk	St. Louis	Row Value
Warehouses In				
Chicago	<u>110</u>	105	<u>80</u>	40
Cincinnati	<u>105</u>	<u>100</u>	75	35
Toledo	130	125	<u>100</u>	60
Pittsburgh	95	<u>90</u>	65	25
Column Value	70	65	40	

This time, when compared with the corresponding rates as shown in CHART I, it is seen that all rates of XIII are equal, or less than, the rates shown on CHART I. Thus, the indicated rates form the optimum shipping schedule for the St. Louis Combination.

The optimum schedules, with their applicable rates and costs are shown in CHART XIV.

CHART XIV

Comparison of Transportation Costs of the Two Proposed Sites

A. St. Louis Site Selected

	Units	Rate	Cost
Houston—Chicago	100	x 1.10	110.00
Houston—Cincinnati	100	x 1.05	105.00
South Norfolk—Cincinnati	200	x 1.00	200.00
South Norfolk—Pittsburgh	150	x .90	135.00
St. Louis—Chicago	250	x .80	200.00
St. Louis—Toledo	200	x 1.00	200.00
Total	1000		950.00

B. Memphis Site Selected

Houston—Chicago	Units	Rate	Cost
Houston—Chicago	200	x 1.10	220.00
South Norfolk—Cincinnati	200	x 1.00	200.00
South Norfolk—Pittsburgh	150	x .90	135.00
Memphis—Chicago	150	x .90	135.00
Memphis—Cincinnati	100	x .70	70.00
Memphis—Toledo	200	x 1.05	210.00
Total	1000		970.00

The reason for completing each schedule becomes clearer by comparing total costs after the completion of each revised schedule. When this is done, it can be seen that Memphis seemingly was ahead of St. Louis after revisions one and two.

	St. Louis	Memphis
Cost of Initial Schedule	$1,110.00	$1,112.50
Cost after 1st Revision	1,045.00	1,030.00
Cost after 2nd Revision	995.00	970.00
Cost after 3rd Revision	950.00	970.00

How important are such savings? Using the restrictions of the problem and computing the savings of $20.00 per operating hour, on a forty-hour week, the annual savings on this one small facet of the companies' overall operations amounts to $41,600.00 annually—nearly $500,000 in the first ten years of operation of the new plant.

In summary, it is evident that to make wise transportation-related decisions (or to understand why certain decisions are made) means that the problem of producing the above type of information on short notice must be anticipated. To meet this demand, the Traffic Executive will require sustained programs to produce new plant information and to check on existing schedules. Needless to say, not only are traffic personnel faced with the task of mastering this and other similar techniques, but if traffic decisions are to be understood then those who would have a need to interpret the impact of traffic decisions must also understand the bases of such decisions.

Bibliography

Chapter 1

ALEXANDER, JOHN W., *Economic Geography*, Englewood Cliffs, New Jersey: Prentice-Hall, Inc., 1963.

FAIR, MARVIN L. and WILLIAMS, ERNEST W., *Economics of Transportation*, New York: Harper and Brothers, 1951.

FROMM, GARY, *Transport Investment and Economic Development*, Washington, D. C.: The Brookings Institute, 1965.

The Interstate Commerce Act, Washington, D. C.: Government Printing Office, 1958.

MOSER, DAVID E., and KRIEBEL, WESLEY R., *Transportation In Agriculture and Business*, Columbia, Missouri: University of Missouri, 1964.

NOURSE, HUGH O., *Regional Economics*, New York: McGraw-Hill Book Company, 1968.

SAMPSON, ROY J. and FARRIS, MARTIN T., *Domestic Transportation*, New York: Houghton Mifflin Company, 1966.

SOULE, GEORGE, *Economic Forces in American History*, New York: William Sloane Associates, Inc., 1952.

Transport Requirements For the Growth of North-West, North America, Vols. I, II and III, House Document No. 176, Washington, D. C.: Government Printing Office, 1961.

ULLMAN, EDWARD L., *American Commodity Flow*, Seattle, Washington: University of Washington Press, 1957.

VAN ZANDT, J. PARKER, *The Geography of World Air Transport*, Washington, D. C.: The Brookings Institute, 1944.

WILSON, G. LLOYD, *Transportation and Communications*, New York: Appleton-Century-Crofts, Inc., 1954.

Chapter 2

International Geographical Union, "Preliminary Report of the Commission on Industrial Ports," New York: 1952.

Chapter 3

BOGART, ERNEST LUDLOW, *Economic History of The American People*, New York: Longmans, Green and Co., 1938.

CHANDLER, ALRED D., JR., *The Railroads: The Nation's First Big Business*, New York: Harcourt, Brace and World, Inc., 1965.

"Common Carrier Capabilities," *Transportation and Distribution Management*, VIII, No. 5, May, 1968, p. 40.

RISTOW, WALTER W., *A Survey of the Roads of the United States of America by 1789*, Cambridge, Massachusetts: Harvard University Press, 1961.

SMITH, SAMUEL V., *The Role of Water Transport in the Industrial Development of the St. Louis Region*, St. Louis, Missouri: Bardgett Printing and Publishing, Washington University, 1957.

"Trends in Transportation Technology," *Handling and Shipping*, IX, No. 3, March, 1968, p. 45.

BECHT, J. EDWIN, "The Chemical Industry and the Midwestern River and Intracoastal Canal Routes," *Waterways*, Vol. XX, No. 1, October, 1955.

———, "New Roads and Their Consequences," *The Houston Business Review*, VII, No. 5, May, 1960, p. 8.

Chapter 4

American Gas Association, *Natural Gas*, (No publication date listed.)

Association of American Railroads, *Railroads of America*, Washington, D. C., 1968.

———, *Transportation In America*, Washington, D. C., 1947.

The American Waterways Operators, Inc., *The Barge and Towing Industry United For Action*, Washington, D. C., 1969.

———, *Big Load Afloat*, Washington, D. C., 1965.

BARRIGER, JOHN WALKER, *Super-Railroads For a Dynamic American Economy*, New York: Simmons-Boardman Publishing Corporation, 1956.

United States Department of Commerce. Maritime Administration. Essential United States Foreign Trade Routes. Washington, D. C.: Government Printing Office, 1957.

WOLBERT, GEORGE S., JR., *American Pipelines*, Norman, Oklahoma: University of Oklahoma Press, 1952.

Chapter 5

ALDERSON, WROE, and SHAPIRO, STANLEY S., *Marketing and the Computer*, Englewood Cliffs, New Jersey: Prentice-Hall, Inc., 1963.

BEER, STAFFORD, *Cybernetics and Management*, New York: John Wiley and Sons, Inc., 1964.

BERRY, BRIAN J. L., *Geography of Market Centers and Retail Distribution*, Englewood Cliffs, New Jersey: Prentice-Hall, Inc., 1967.

ISARD, WALTER, *Location and Space Economy*, New York: John Wiley and Sons, Inc., 1956.

———, *Methods of Regional Analysis*, New York: John Wiley and Sons, Inc., 1960.

LOCKLIN, PHILIP D., *Economics of Transportation*, Homewood, Illinois: Richard D. Irwin, Inc., 1960.

LÖSCH, AUGUST, *The Economics of Location*, New Haven, Conn.: Yale University Press, 1954.

OWEN, WILFRED, *The Metropolitan Transportation Problem*, Washington, D. C.: The Brookings Institute, 1966.

PERLE, EUGENE D., *The Demand For Transportation: Region and Commodity Studies In the United States*, Chicago, Illinois: The University of Chicago Press, 1964.

PERLMAN, A. E., *Association of American Railroads Delegation to Symposium on Cybernetics, Paris, France,* Association of American Railroads, Washington, D. C., 1963.

WARNER, DANIE S., *Marketing and Distribution,* New York: McGraw-Hill Book Company, 1969.

Chapter 6

"Airlines: Building a Total Travel Market," *The Marketing Magazine,* June 1, 1967, p. 15.

BECKER, H. G., JR., "A National Distribution Pattern Second to None," *Handling and Shipping,* IX, No. 10, October, 1968, p. 53.

BOWERSOX, DONALD J., LALONDE, BERNARD J., and SMYKAY, EDWARD W., *Physical Distribution Management,* Toronto, Ontario. The Macmillan Company, 1969.

Committee on Commerce, United States Senate, *National Transportation Policy,* Washington, D. C.: Government Printing Office, 1961.

COVER, VIRGIL D. (Editor), *The Dynamic Role of Physical Distribution Management.* Proceedings of the Eighteenth Annual Transportation Conference, Syracuse, New York: Syracuse University, November 7, 1966.

HARMON, GEORGE M., *Coordination of Service,* Proceedings of the Sixteenth Annual Transportation Conference, Syracuse, N. Y.: Syracuse University, 1964.

HESKETT, J. L., IVIE, ROBERT M., and GLASKOWSKY, NICHOLAS A., JR., *Business Logistics,* New York: The Ronald Press, 1964.

HOOVER, EDGAR M., *The Location of Economic Activity,* New York: McGraw-Hill Book Company, Inc., 1948.

MAGEE, JOHN F., *Physical Distribution Systems,* New York: McGraw-Hill Book Company, 1967.

MCELHINEY, PAUL T., and HILTON, CHARLES L., *Introduction to Logistics and Traffic Management,* Dubuque, Iowa: Wm. C. Brown Company, Publishers, 1968.

MOSSMAN, FRANK H., and MORTON, NEWTON, *Logistics of Distribution Systems,* Boston: Allyn and Bacon, Inc., 1965.

OVERMYER, D. H., "The Intermodal Terminal Complex," *Handling and Shipping,* IX, No. 12, December, 1968, p. 34.

OWEN, WILFRED, *The Metropolitan Transportation Problem,* Washington, D. C.: The Brookings Institute, 1966.

PEGRUM, DUDLEY F., *Conflicts in Transport,* Proceedings 20th Annual Meeting, American Society of Traffic and Transportation, Los Angeles, California, September 8-9, 1965.

PLOWMAN, E. GROSVENOR, *Elements of Business Logistics,* Stanford, California: Stanford University, 1964.

RUPPENTHAL, KARL M., *Issues in Transportation Economics,* Columbus, Ohio: Charles E. Merrill Books, Inc., 1965.

SIMS, E. RALPH, JR., "Commerce, Containers and Foreign Policy," *Handling and Shipping,* IX, No. 3, March, 1968, p. 45.

TAYLOR, ROBERT M. and MARKS, NORTON E., *Marketing Logistics: Perspectives and Viewpoints,* 1967.

Index

A GEOGRAPHY OF

transportation and
business logistics

WM. C. BROWN COMPANY PUBLISHERS
Dubuque, Iowa